NATIONAL
GEOGRAPHIC

POCKET GUIDE TO THE
Weather
OF NORTH AMERICA

POCKET GUIDE TO THE
Weather
OF NORTH AMERICA

JACK WILLIAMS

NATIONAL GEOGRAPHIC

WASHINGTON, D.C.

CONTENTS

Introduction 6

||||||||||||||||||||||||||||||||||||||||||||||||||||||||||||||||||||||||||||||

||||||||||||||||||||||||||||||||||||||||||||||||||||||||||||||||||||||||||||||

Weather

Nature You Can't Ignore

Most of the time, people go about their daily lives without thinking much about the weather. Before they leave home for the day, a brief radio forecast or a glance at a website tells them all they need to know: How should I dress to go out for the day? Many people, however, are fascinated by the ever-changing sky and weather, and they want to keep on learning about it.

A Quick Guide to Weather Science

Our day-to-day weather is the result of the sun's unequal heating of Earth, with the tropics—the belt circling Earth 1,600 miles (2,575 km) north and south of the Equator—receiving much more solar energy than the regions around the North and South Poles. Storms and ocean currents along with calmer winds move warm and cold air and water, redistributing heat, balancing Earth's heat budget. These movements of warm and cold air create our day-to-day weather.

While Earth sees relatively great temperature extremes, the range of temperatures allows some forms of life over almost all of the planet. Earth's monthly average temperatures range from as cold as -80°F (-62°C) on Antarctica's polar plateau to 100°F (38°C) on tropical deserts. The world's single-day lowest temperature ever officially recorded was -129°F (-89.4°C) at the Russian Vostok Station in Antarctica on July 21, 1983, during the coldest part of the Southern Hemisphere winter. Earth's single hottest daily temperature on record is 134°F (56.7°C) at Furnace Creek, California, on July 10, 1913, at what is now the headquarters of Death Valley National Park.

By the way, on January 8, 1913, Furnace Creek set its cold temperature record, 15°F (-9.4°C). Furnace Creek has tied this temperature since then, but has never been colder. This tells us something about desert climates: Temperatures drop rapidly after sunset because such dry climates have little water

BECOMING INVOLVED WITH WEATHER

The books, websites, and organizations in "Further Resources" will help you to learn more about weather and climate. If you want to look into becoming a meteorologist, or otherwise become directly involved with weather, you have various possibilities.

+ If you like to watch storms and want to learn more about them and help the U.S. National Weather Service, you should consider becoming one of more than 290,000 trained volunteers who send reports of severe weather to a local NWS office. To become involved, contact the Warning Coordination Meteorologist at your local NWS office and arrange to take the training course these offices offer. To do this, go to www.stormready.noaa.gov/contact.shtml and follow the directions. You will learn the basics of safety.

You can also check with your local weather office about becoming a volunteer cooperative weather observer. Since 1890, volunteers in this program have been sending data from NWS instruments on their property—mostly temperature and precipitation—to the NWS. These data are used to supplement climate reports from places away from NWS and other official weather stations.

+ The Community Collaborative Rain, Hail and Snow Network is looking for volunteer observers to add to its thousands of volunteers. It is now the largest provider of daily precipitation observations in the United States, and has moved into Canada. Information is available at www.cocorahs.org. Becoming an observer is a good way to learn about weather.

+ Environment Canada's Meteorological Service has a storm spotter program called the Canadian Weather Amateur Radio Network, which began as a program for amateur radio operators but now is open to anyone who wants to be a storm spotter. Contact your nearest Environment Canada weather office for information.

+ The U.S. National Oceanic and Atmospheric Administration (NOAA)—the parent agency of the National Weather Service—offers a free smartphone app that enables anyone to report precipitation anonymously. Anyone can use the app to report storms to researchers at NOAA's Severe Storms Laboratory and the University of Oklahoma. NOAA and the university are using the reports to build a database. The reports are not used for warnings.

vapor in the air to absorb heat radiating away from the ground and radiate it back down.

Atmosphere & Water

If Earth didn't have an atmosphere and oceans, the planet's daily temperatures would probably be much like those on the moon, which range from mean daytime highs of approximately 260°F (127°C) and overnight lows of -280°F (-173°C). Copious amounts of water are important for Earth's weather, and not just because water fills the oceans. Water is the raw material for clouds—and all kinds of

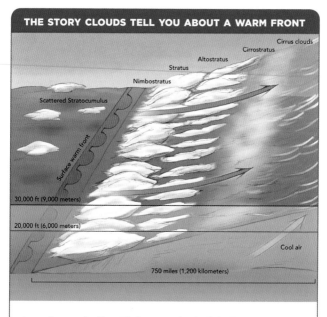

THE STORY CLOUDS TELL YOU ABOUT A WARM FRONT

Cirrus clouds
Cirrostratus
Altostratus
Stratus
Nimbostratus
Scattered Stratocumulus
Surface warm front
30,000 ft (9,000 meters)
20,000 ft (6,000 meters)
Cool air
750 miles (1,200 kilometers)

As you become familiar with the various kinds of clouds you can use this new knowledge to help you see the bigger weather picture of weather changes and movements. Here you see a cross section of a typical warm front. The succession of clouds shown here could take maybe 24 to 36 hours from the time you see cirrus clouds high in the sky until the sur-face warm front has passed.

A thundercloud builds before a storm at Fort Whyte Centre in Winnipeg, Manitoba.

precipitation. Without water, Earth's weather would be like that currently on Mars: It would feature winds blowing dust around and wide temperature changes.

Water Supplies Storm Energy

In addition to supplying raw material for clouds and precipitation, water supplies some of the energy that powers the weather. Water is the only natural substance that exists in all three states of matter—solid, liquid, and gas—at temperatures and pressures found near Earth's surface. When it changes among its phases, water either takes in energy as heat from the surrounding air, which cools the air, or adds heat to the surrounding air, warming it.

Heat is taken from the surroundings when water evaporates into vapor, when ice melts into water, or when ice sublimates directly to water vapor without first melting. This is why evaporation of perspiration from our skin cools us in hot weather. If the air is too humid for perspiration to evaporate easily, we become sticky and hot.

The air's invisible water vapor contains energy to power violent weather such as this summer storm building over Florida's Everglades.

Heat taken from the surroundings is called latent heat. When water vapor condenses into liquid water or deposits directly to ice, it returns its latent heat to the surroundings, as does water when it freezes into ice. Condensation, deposition, and freezing all add energy to the surrounding air, warming it. Energy added to rising air by condensation, deposition, and freezing adds heat to the air, making the heat rise faster and farther. Such latent heat releases the supply of energy for thunderstorms and hurricanes.

As air descends, as when falling rain drags it down, it warms, causing water to evaporate and ice to melt into water or sublimate directly into water vapor. These processes take energy from the falling air, making it colder and thus heavier. Normally, sinking air warms, but the heat taken away by water's phase changes more than offsets this warming. Under the right conditions, the air grows cool and heavy enough to smash into the ground as a damaging microburst during a shower or thunderstorm.

Stable & Unstable Atmospheres

Meteorologists use the words "stable" and "unstable" in a technical sense to describe what kind of weather to expect at particular times and places. Nevertheless, the words carry similar connotations when used to describe people. A "stable" person is one who stays calm even under pressure. When the atmosphere is stable, you might have rain or snow, but it will fall over a wide area without thunderstorms. An "unstable" person reacts with road rage when another driver gets in the way. When the atmosphere is unstable, the weather can produce strong thunderstorms, maybe even tornadoes.

When the atmosphere is stable, air that is given an upward shove (as by wind blowing upward on a mountain) will stop rising and begin sinking when the shove stops. In an unstable atmosphere, the air continues rising after the shove ceases. The temperature profile of the atmosphere makes the difference. Rising air cools by 3.56°F for each 1,000 feet (1.98°C/305 m) of altitude gained. When water vapor begins evaporating, it releases latent heat, warming the air, which offsets the cooling to some degree. This means humid air can rise farther and faster than dry air.

Here's how this works. If the temperature is 60°F (15.5°C) at the surface, a bubble of air will cool to 56.5°F (13.6°C) when it rises 1,000 feet. If the temperature of the surrounding air here is 53°F (11.7°C), the bubble will be warmer. It will continue rising. The atmosphere here is unstable. When the bubble becomes colder than the surrounding air, it stops rising; the atmosphere at this height is stable. Forecasters need to know the stability to make predictions.

What Causes the Seasons?

Earth's North Pole–South Pole axis tilts 23.5° in relation to its yearly path around the sun. This tilt causes the seasons, by changing the distribution of sunlight throughout the year.

KEY FACTS

Seasons are formed by the tilt of Earth on its axis, which causes unequal sunshine in various regions of Earth.

+ fact: On the equinoxes—March 19–21, and Sept. 22–23—the sun is directly above the Equator.

+ fact: On the Dec. 21–22 solstice—Northern Hemisphere winter—the sun is directly above the Tropic of Capricorn, latitude 23.5° S.

On September 22 or 23, the sun shines equally on all of Earth. Until December 21 or 22, days grow shorter in the Northern Hemisphere as the sun moves higher in the sky and days grow longer south of the Equator. On December 21 or 22, the winter solstice, the sun never rises north of latitude 66.5° N (the Arctic Circle); it never sets south of latitude 66.5° S (the Antarctic Circle). This process reverses until March 19, 20, or 21, when the sun again shines equally on all of Earth. Until June 20 or 21 the Southern Hemisphere receives less sun, turning colder as the Northern Hemisphere receives more sun and warms up.

March 20

June 21

Dec 21

Sept 23

Climate Zones

The amount of solar energy any part of Earth receives determines whether it will have a tropical, temperate, or polar climate. A location's elevation and nearness to an ocean also affect climate.

KEY FACTS

A region's climate depends on the latitude.

+ fact: Tropical climates have average temperatures above 64°F (18°C).

+ fact: Temperate climates have four seasons without extreme temperatures.

+ fact: Polar climates have no monthly averages higher than 50°F (10°C). On some days the sun never sets; on others it never rises.

Climate is the long-term average weather of an area, including temperatures and precipitation. The tropics, zones immediately north and south of the Equator, receive the most solar energy: The sun is almost directly overhead all year, and so on average the tropics are Earth's warmest region. The polar regions, centered on the North and South Poles, receive the least amount of solar energy because the sun is always low in the sky, and it doesn't come up at all for part of the year in some regions. On average, these are Earth's coldest regions. In between, the temperate zones have variable climates without widespread tropical or polar extremes.

Tropic of Cancer 23° 26' N
Equator
Tropic of Capricorn 23° 26' S

Heat Balance

To a large degree, atmospheric winds and oceanic currents even out the temperature contrasts caused by day and night, and the seasonal variations caused by Earth's tilted axis.

KEY FACTS

Without oceans and atmosphere, Earth's temperatures would be like the moon's, which drop by hundreds of degrees after sunset.

+ fact: Winds aloft and at Earth's surface move warm air toward the poles, cool air toward the Equator.

+ fact: Ocean-top currents carry warm water toward the poles; underwater currents haul cold water toward the Equator.

In the tropics, warm, humid air rises, forming towering Intertropical Convergence Zone thunderstorms. Air flowing in to replace the rising air creates tropical trade winds above the oceans. Air from the storms moves toward the south or north, but Earth's rotation upsets this simple, theoretical pattern. Earth's complex wind patterns include high-altitude jet streams and air sinking at some places, rising at others. These winds and the water vapor they carry are major drivers of storms, warm and cold outbreaks, and other weather events. Human activity may alter these naturally occurring events.

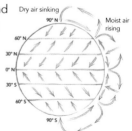

Dry air sinking
90° N
Moist air rising
60° N
30° N
0° N
30° S
60° S
90° S

How Humans Affect the Weather

Earth's average overall temperature changes slowly and has warmed and cooled in the past. It is now warming, with greenhouse gases added to the air by human activity playing an important role.

KEY FACTS

Without the natural greenhouse effect, Earth's average temperature would be 0°F (-19°C).

+ fact: Many prefer the phrase "climate change" because warming caused by added greenhouse gases is only one phenomenon now occurring.

+ fact: Greenhouse gas emissions are falling in developed countries but are rising in developing nations.

Climate scientists are unwilling to say that climate change caused any particular weather event, such as a hurricane or heat wave, but evidence is strong that the Earth is warming faster than it would without human-related causes, especially by added greenhouse gases, which trap heat that would otherwise escape. The number of local record high temperatures is increasing while record low temperatures are decreasing.

Globally, glaciers are shrinking, and ice on lakes and rivers is breaking up earlier in the spring. Some of the biggest changes are happening in the Arctic, where sea ice is shrinking. Scientists in the past had frequently predicted that many of the changes we are now experiencing would eventually occur.

Cloud Composition and Colors

Clouds are made of tiny water drops or ice crystals held up by rising air. Rain or snow falls when the drops or crystals grow large enough to overcome the resistance of rising air.

KEY FACTS

The faster air rises into clouds, the bigger the drops or crystals can grow before they begin falling.

+ fact: Air rises as slowly as inches an hour in some clouds, faster than 100 mph (160 kph) in others.

+ fact: The lowest clouds touch the ground as fog; the highest can reach above 60,000 ft (18,200 m).

The water drops and ice crystals that make up clouds are large enough to scatter all wavelengths of sunlight, which makes the tops and sunny sides of clouds white. Bottoms of thin clouds are also white. Dark cloud bottoms don't necessarily mean rain. At least half of the sunlight hitting a cloud less than 3,000 feet (roughly 900 m) deep makes it through the cloud. This causes many cloud bottoms to be gray while the tops and sides facing the sun are white. Little sunlight passes through clouds more than 3,000 feet deep, which makes their bottoms dark. Shadows of other clouds also darken clouds. Sunrise and sunset turn clouds yellow, orange, or red.

Creating Clouds

Clouds form when rising air becomes cold enough for the air's humidity to begin turning into cloud drops or ice crystals and interact with particles in the air.

KEY FACTS

The temperature of the surrounding air does not affect the cooling rate of rising air.

+ fact: When condensation begins, water vapor releases heat, which reduces rising air's cooling rate to less than 4.5°F per 1,000 ft (1.98°C per 305 m).

+ fact: Air is rising in all clouds at speeds ranging from inches an hour in many clouds to 100 mph (160 kph) in fierce thunderstorms.

Even when rising air is cool enough for water vapor to begin condensing into cloud drops, the vapor needs help. Condensation begins with water vapor molecules attaching to tiny particles in the air known as cloud condensation nuclei. Sometimes called cloud seeds, these nuclei include dust and a variety of other natural substances as well as some kinds of pollution.

Satellite images show long, bright clouds created by nuclei from ship-exhaust gases. These illustrate how added nuclei create many tiny cloud drops that reflect more light than nearby ordinary clouds with larger drops. This is one illustration of the complexities of clouds and why scientists continue working diligently to learn more about these important phenomena.

Cloud Names

Today, with a few additions and enhancements, we still use a Latin-based system of cloud names devised in the early 1800s and adopted internationally.

KEY FACTS

Latin words borrowed for cloud names are *cumulus*, meaning "heap"; *stratus*, "layer"; *cirrus*, "wispy"; and *nimbus*, "rain."

+ fact: Cloud names can be combined into a new word, as in cumulonimbus and cirrostratus, or into a "species" name, such as cumulus congestus.

+ fact: Meteorologists added "alto" for middle-level clouds.

Scientist Luke Howard organized clouds much as the 18th-century Swedish biologist Carl Linnaeus had devised the system of genus and species for plants and animals. A British chemist whose company manufactured medications, Howard practiced meteorology on his own. He first presented his cloud system during an 1802 lecture in London, which was widely publicized and accepted by those developing the science of meteorology. Howard's decision to incorporate Latin into his naming system, as Linnaeus had done with biology, helped make the names international. At the time, scientists were beginning to figure out how clouds form and their importance in understanding weather. Howard's focus on clouds as visible indications of atmospheric changes helped advance the science.

Describing Cloud Cover

Meteorologists use specific terms for the general public and different ones for pilots to describe how much of the sky clouds cover currently or are forecast to cover.

KEY FACTS

+ fact: Clouds cover ⅛ to ¼ of sky. For pilots: few clouds; for public: mostly clear at night, mostly sunny in daytime.

+ fact: Clouds cover ⅜ to ½ of sky. For pilots: scattered clouds; for public: partly cloudy.

+ fact: Clouds cover ⅝ to ⅞ of sky. For pilots: broken clouds; for public: mostly cloudy or considerable cloudiness.

Although the terms "scattered" and "partly cloudy" mean the same thing, as shown in Key Facts, the U.S. National Weather Service uses "scattered" in communications for pilots and "partly cloudy" for the public, and you might hear both. Pilots and air traffic controllers also need to know how far above the ground the bottoms of the clouds are. Weather stations have automated ceilometers, which send pulses of infrared light straight up and measure the time needed to reflect back to the instrument to calculate cloud heights. Each minute, the instrument uses the last 30 minutes of data on when clouds were above it to calculate cloud cover. For pilots and the public, "overcast" refers to clouds covering more than seven-eighths of the sky. Gradually increasing cloudiness can show that rain or snow is coming.

Cumuliform Clouds

Puffy cumulus clouds form in an unstable atmosphere humid enough for its water to condense into cloud drops in bubbles of warm air rising as narrow streams called thermals.

KEY FACTS

Water vapor begins condensing when air cools to its dew point temperature. Humid air has a higher dew point.

+ fact: Condensing water vapor releases the heat it gained when it evaporated, which warms the air, making it rise farther and faster.

+ fact: Growing cumulus clouds have flat bottoms at the height where condensation begins.

Meteorologists say the atmosphere at a particular time and place is unstable when rising air, which always cools at a steady rate, stays warmer—thus lighter—than the surrounding air. It continues in this direction—at times to great heights—as long as the rising air remains warmer than the surrounding air. Relatively warm air at the surface and cold air aloft creates instability. As air is rising to form cumulus clouds, some air aloft is sinking around the clouds, keeping the air between clouds clear. These up-and-down air movements—termed "convection"—form individual cumulus clouds of various sizes instead of a single, widespread cloud covering a large area.

Stratiform Clouds

Stratiform clouds form in a stable atmosphere that doesn't support cumuliform thermals because air doesn't continue rising after the initial shove upward.

Meteorologists say the atmosphere at a particular time and place is stable when rising air, which always cools at a steady rate, grows colder—thus heavier—than the surrounding air. Once the air becomes heavier than the surrounding air, it will stop rising, which means cumulus clouds cannot form. Stratiform clouds form when all of the air in a particular area is pushed up, such as when wind carries warm air up and over heavier cold air at the surface. As stable air is pushed up, it spreads out to form a layer or layers of stratiform clouds that are thinner but wider than cumulus clouds.

Orographic Clouds

Rain or snow falling from orographic clouds are important sources of water for many regions, including much of the western United States.

KEY FACTS

When the atmosphere is stable, air continues rising as it reaches mountaintops and can create thunderstorms.

+ fact: When the atmosphere is unstable, air flowing over mountains forms turbulent rising and sinking that can stretch 100 mi (160 km) or more.

+ fact: Arid regions downstream of large mountains are called rain shadows.

When humid winds blow over hills or mountains, orographic clouds form. In some locations, these clouds bring most of the year's snow and rain. Air flowing up mountains cools enough for its humidity to condense into raindrops or to form snow. This orographic precipitation waters trees and other plants that cover mountains, even while nearby lower elevations remain arid. Spring and summer melting of mountain snow feeds rivers, fills reservoirs, and becomes the major source of water for places far from the mountains. In the Sierra Nevada and Cascades ranges of the West, for example, flowing air loses moisture over the mountains, creating the dry Great Basin east of the mountains.

Cirrus Clouds

Wispy white cirrus clouds make for a painterly sky. Formed at high altitudes and composed mostly of ice crystals, they can signal light snow or rain.

KEY FACTS

Cirrus clouds block little sunlight but absorb infrared radiation from Earth, contributing to the greenhouse effect.

+ fact: Cirrus clouds are made mostly of ice crystals—they are located in -50°F (-46°C) air.

+ fact: At any one time, cirrus clouds cover approximately 25 percent of the Earth.

Cirrus clouds form when water vapor that has been pumped high into the air, often by a storm, turns directly into ice crystals—a process called deposition. Cirrus clouds can be a sign that rain or snow is on the way, maybe in a day or so. The only precipitation these clouds produce is light snow, which evaporates long before reaching the ground. Meteorologists identify these wisps of snow as "fall streaks," but they are commonly called "mares' tails." Some cirrus clouds are as thin as roughly 300 feet (100 m); others are as thick as 5,000 feet (1,500 m). Cirrus clouds are white—except around sunrise and sunset—and are generally transparent.

Nacreous Clouds

Nacreous clouds form in the stratosphere high above the Arctic and Antarctic, where they help to destroy stratospheric ozone. They are sometimes, but very rarely, seen at lower latitudes.

KEY FACTS

Destruction of stratospheric ozone is a concern because it blocks harmful ultraviolet radiation.

+ fact: Nacreous clouds are 49,000–82,000 ft (15,000–25,000 m) high, where temperatures are below -108°F (-78°C).

+ fact: They are named for iridescent nacre, a material that some mollusks make that is also know as mother of pearl.

Nacreous clouds can be seen from the northern regions of Europe, Asia, and North America and over Antarctica, but they are very rarely seen elsewhere. Little was known about them until 1982, when NASA scientists using satellite data described them in detail, including the fact that they form regularly over Antarctica in the ozone layer and sometimes over the Arctic. The researchers named them "polar stratospheric clouds." In 1986 and 1987, scientists working in Antarctica found that these clouds are, in effect, natural laboratories that enable human-made substances including chlorofluorocarbons (such as Freon) to destroy stratospheric ozone. Temperatures over Antarctica are low enough for the clouds to form every winter, but they form only occasionally over the Arctic.

Cirrocumulus Clouds

Cirrocumulus clouds are white patches of high cloud without gray shadows and with lumps called cloudlets, often a sign that rain or snow could arrive in a day or sooner.

KEY FACTS

Cirrocumulus clouds are the least common high clouds.

+ fact: Cirrocumulus cloudlets appear to be the size of the tip of your little finger held at arm's length (or smaller).

+ fact: Cirrocumulus clouds are mostly ice crystals but often include liquid drops that have not frozen in well-below-freezing air.

Cirrocumulus clouds are usually found higher than 20,000 feet (6,100 m). If you watch one for a while, you might see it turn into a cirrostratus or cirrus cloud or dissipate—because any particular cirrocumulus cloud tends to have a short life. The cloudlets show that convection—up-and-down air movement—is occurring, as it is in any cloud with "cumulus" as part of its name.

These clouds are usually in relatively warm air that is moving over cooler, denser air. Cirrocumulus take shape at a distance of maybe 500 miles (800 km) or more ahead of a warm front, which is the surface boundary between warm and cold air.

Cirrostratus Clouds

Cirrostratus clouds are high clouds, above 20,000 feet (6,100 m). They are sometimes too thin to hide the sun or moon, even though they might be as much as 1,000 feet (305 m) thick.

KEY FACTS

Some very thin cirrostratus clouds appear only as a halo around the sun or moon.

+ fact: Forecasters use "hazy sunshine," to describe the milky look of the sky with cirrostratus clouds.

+ fact: Fibrous cirrostratus clouds with no halos are called "cirrostratus fibratus."

Cirrostratus clouds are made of ice crystals and are generally thin and uniform. They form when warm air moving over heavier cold air ahead of a warm front or rising air in the center of a surface low-pressure area lifts humid air into the upper atmosphere. If you see them replace cirrus clouds over a few hours and then grow thick enough to hide the sun or moon, you know snow or rain has a good chance of arriving within 24 hours— and maybe sooner. Just as other high clouds do, cirrostratus clouds frequently reflect red and yellow patterns that create spectacular sunrises and sunsets.

Contrails

Contrails are long, thin clouds that form behind high-flying airplanes as water vapor in the airplane's engine exhaust creates a narrow stream of air humid enough for a cloud to form.

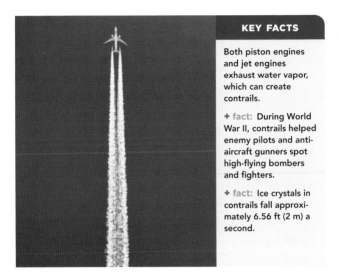

KEY FACTS

Both piston engines and jet engines exhaust water vapor, which can create contrails.

+ fact: During World War II, contrails helped enemy pilots and anti-aircraft gunners spot high-flying bombers and fighters.

+ fact: Ice crystals in contrails fall approximately 6.56 ft (2 m) a second.

"Contrail" is short for "condensation trail," which ia a narrow cloud of condensed water vapor that becomes visible behind airplanes flying higher than 26,000 feet (8,000 m), where the temperature is colder than approximately -40°F (-40°C). Water vapor in the airplane's exhaust added to the air's own water vapor transforms into ice crystals around nuclei of material including particles in the exhaust. Contrails grow long when the air at their altitude is humid, a phenomenon that can indicate rain or snow is on the way. Minimal contrails behind a high-flying airplane means the air at its altitude is dry; so contrails barely form or they quickly evaporate. When contrails persist for more than a few minutes, winds aloft often push them into wavy paths.

Altocumulus Clouds

These puffy clouds, white and gray with darker patches, generally form about 6,500 to 20,000 feet (2,000 to 6,100 m) above the ground and can cover large areas of the sky.

KEY FACTS

Altocumulus clouds on warm, humid mornings indicate thunderstorms that day.

+ fact: Individual clouds appear as wide as your thumb with your hand at arm's length.

+ fact: A sky with wavy, mixed altocumulus and cirrocumulus clouds and blue-sky gaps is called a "mackerel sky" because it resembles fish scales.

Altocumulus clouds form in various ways. They might develop from cumulus clouds that grow to an altitude where rising air slows and spreads out, or they might be transformations of other clouds including altostratus, stratocumulus, or nimbostratus. The clouds are usually made of water drops, although ice sometimes is found. They are usually less than 3,000 feet (roughly 900 m) thick and sometimes produce virga—rain that evaporates on the way down—but they rarely produce rain that reaches the ground. They may form distinct layers or parallel bands of clouds, called cloud streets, with air rising into the clouds and sinking between the bands.

Undulatus Asperatus Clouds

Since 2009, news reports have suggested that this is a new variety of cloud. Although sightings of such clouds are rare, there is no reason to think they are new.

KEY FACTS

Billow clouds are the undulatus variety you are most likely to see, often with a blue-sky background.

+ fact: Gavin Pretor-Pinney, founder of the Cloud Appreciation Society in the U.K., suggested the cloud's name.

+ fact: Undulatus clouds highlight the atmosphere's many natural wavy motions

An "undulatus" cloud, according to the American Meteorological Society glossary, is composed of long, parallel elements, merged or separate, that look like undulating ocean waves. The term "asperatus" comes from the Latin verb for "rough or difficult." Margaret LeMone, a scientist at the National Center for Atmospheric Research, recalls taking her first photo of such a cloud "on a wintry day in Columbia, Missouri, probably in the 1970s," and says she has seen others since then. Is it a new type? Maybe, instead, this cloud reminds us that if you look at enough clouds, you're bound to see some that are hard to classify. If you continue closely observing clouds, you'll learn that such ambiguity is common. This is a reason why many people find the sky and weather fascinating.

Lenticular Clouds

You're a few miles from a mountain or mountain range and see something like a flying saucer. You are almost surely looking at a lenticular cloud formed by wind blowing over mountains.

KEY FACTS

Lens-shaped clouds atop mountains, sometimes stacked up, are called "mountain wave clouds."

+ fact: Airline pilots avoid mountain wave turbulence, but pilots of sailplanes use the waves to climb above 50,000 ft (15,000 m).

+ fact: Lenticular clouds are most common east of the Sierra Nevada and the Rockies.

When the atmosphere is stable, wind goes down and up in a wavy pattern after it has crossed mountains. (When it is unstable, the air keeps rising.) Unless the air is very dry, a lens-shaped cloud or line of clouds forms atop the wave or waves. Air rising toward the top of a wave cools, and its humidity condenses into cloud drops. Air descending from the top of a wave warms, which evaporates cloud drops. The combined processes create this lens-shaped cloud. Lenticular clouds change shape little and stay the same distance from the mountains instead of traveling downstream with the winds. These clouds remain stationary as air moves through them.

Mammatus Clouds

Mammatus clouds are pouches that hang from the bottoms of clouds, most commonly from a thunderstorm anvil, a cloud spreading out from the storm's top.

KEY FACTS

"Mammatus" comes from the Latin word *mamma*—meaning "udder" or "breast."

+ fact: While mammatus clouds are most common on thunderstorm anvils, they also appear rarely under altocumulus, altostratus, and cirrus clouds, and even contrails.

+ fact: Most clouds form in rising air; mammatus clouds form in sinking air.

Mammatus pouches, which can be transparent or opaque, form when blobs of cold air containing water drops, ice crystals, or both begin sinking into clear air below a cloud. They descend into increasing air pressure, which warms the falling drops and crystals. At the same time, the crystals or drops are evaporating into water vapor, which cools them, offsetting the warming to some extent and keeping them cooler, thus heavier, than the surrounding air. The blob of crystals or drops sinks below the bottom of the cloud and looks like a pouch. Individual pouches may last 10 minutes, but a cluster can last for hours.

||||||||||||||||||||||||||||||||||||||||||||||||||||||||||||||||||||||||||||||||||||||||||

Altocumulus Castellanus Clouds

Altocumulus castellanus clouds look somewhat like the turrets
of a castle. If you see these early in the day, it could signal rain or
thunderstorms later that day.

KEY FACTS

Tall, narrow castellanus clouds are called turkey necks.

+ fact: These can show that rising air is breaking through a warm layer that has been suppressing thunderstorms.

+ fact: Castellanus towers are easier to see from the side rather than along the narrow cloud's length.

When rolls of altocumulus clouds begin sprouting towers, the atmosphere above the clouds is becoming unstable enough that they might grow into towering cumulus and possibly thunderstorms that day. Such instability means the atmosphere above altocumulus clouds is cold enough for rising air to stay warmer than the surrounding air and continue rising. The towers are not a guarantee of thunderstorms, just a possible predictor. If the air near the ground is humid, thunderstorms are more likely. If you are on an airplane about to take off with castellanus clouds overhead, expect some turbulence as the airplane flies through the clouds.

Stratocumulus Clouds

Like other kinds of stratiform clouds, stratocumulus clouds spread across large areas with small breaks between individual clouds. In addition, they display a rounded cumuliform shape.

KEY FACTS

Stratocumulus clouds cover an average of 23 percent of the oceans and 12 percent of land.

+ fact: Individual stratocumulus clouds appear roughly the size of your fist when you extend your arm full length toward the cloud.

+ fact: Stratocumulus clouds produce little precipitation—mostly drizzle, light rain, or snow.

Stratocumulus clouds are most common over chilly oceans in the subtropics where air is slowly sinking from aloft, warming it. The layer of warm air blocks humid air from rising far from cool oceans. Thus, stratocumulus clouds generally don't rise above 8,000 feet (2,400 m). Stratocumulus clouds also form over land where air is descending into a surface high-pressure area and warming. If cumulus clouds are forming in such an area, they stop growing taller at the warm layer and spread out. Because the tops of stratocumulus clouds reflect a good share of the sunlight that hits them, they tend to cool the Earth.

Stratus Clouds

Stratus clouds are featureless gray layers with generally uniform bases. They sometimes, but rarely, produce drizzle, small ice crystals, and snow grains.

KEY FACTS

Instead of rain or snow, drizzle, snow grains, or tiny ice crystals usually fall from stratus clouds.

+ fact: A stratus fractus cloud has parts of different sizes and brightness that change rapidly.

+ fact: When you can see the sun through the clouds, its outline is usually clearly discernible.

Stratus clouds are common in coastal areas because the air contains abundant humidity at low levels and the atmosphere is likely to be stable, which favors their development. Fog moving in from the ocean at night can set the stage. Stratus clouds sometimes form when the bottom of a layer of fog evaporates, and the lower part of the fog rises off the ground. Stratocumulus clouds can also form into stratus when the bottom of the stratocumulus descends and spreads out under a layer of warm air aloft. Stratus clouds are most common at night and in the early morning, before the sun begins to evaporate them. Stratus clouds can form in air moving into thunderstorms.

Nimbostratus Clouds

When dark, gloomy nimbostratus clouds move in with their steady rain or snow, they leave no doubt that you are in for a period of wet weather and no sun.

KEY FACTS

An altostratus becomes a nimbostratus cloud if it totally blocks the sun or its precipitation reaches the ground.

+ fact: Unattached cloud fragments called "pannus" or "scud" clouds often form below nimbostratus, cumulus, and cumulonimbus clouds.

+ fact: Nimbostratus clouds do not bring lightning, thunder, or hail.

Nimbostratus clouds are low clouds that hang below 6,500 feet (2,000 m) above ground level. They can be a few thousand feet thick and are heavy with suspended water drops, possibly ice crystals, and falling rain or snow that is likely to last for several hours or even more than a day. Little or no sunlight makes it through the cloud. The rain or snow from a nimbostratus is steady, and it falls at a light or moderate rate, not the on-and-off but sometimes drenching rain showers that cumulonimbus clouds produce. The bottoms of nimbostratus clouds tend to be ragged instead of well defined.

Altostratus Clouds

Given their name because they are the highest (alto-) of the stratus or sheet-type clouds, the thin, gray altostratus sky cover signifies a storm could be on the way.

KEY FACTS

Not enough sunlight passes through altostratus clouds to cast shadows on the ground.

+ fact: Altostratus clouds tend to be translucent; you can often see a watery sun or moon through them.

+ fact: A watery moon appearing and disappearing through altostratus clouds is a classic horror movie scene.

If the sky is covered as far as you can see by gray or blue-gray clouds that are 6,000 to 20,000 feet (1,800 to 6,100 m) above the ground, they are altostratus clouds. If the clouds are white or have areas of white, you are instead looking at cirrostratus clouds. Altostratus clouds are made of ice crystals, usually near the top of the cloud, and water drops, near the bottom. They usually arrive ahead of storms that carry widespread, steady rain or snow. As rain or snow continues falling from the altostratus, the cloud's bottom can sink below 6,000 feet, and it becomes a nimbostratus cloud.

Fair-weather Cumulus Clouds

These small, puffy, white clouds portend calm, dry weather for the immediate future, at least early in the day. As the day goes on, they can grow into thunderstorm clouds.

KEY FACTS

The scientific name for fair-weather cumulus clouds is *cumulus humilis*, from the Latin word for "low, lowly, small, or shallow."

+ fact: If you're on an airplane taking off under fair-weather cumulus clouds, expect mild turbulence until you're above the clouds.

+ fact: Fair-weather cumulus commonly form under cirrostratus clouds.

Fair-weather cumulus develop as the sun warms the ground, creating thermals that rise until water vapor begins condensing. Warm air aloft, or air aloft that cools too slowly with height, blocks air from rising higher than the cloud tops. If this continues, the day will remain calm. If you see one or a few clouds growing higher than the others, you know that either air is rising into them with enough force to break through the warm layer, or that the atmosphere above the clouds has cooled, making it more unstable. When this happens, one or a few of the smaller cumulus clouds can grow into cumulus congestus (page 38) and even thunderstorms.

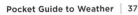

Cumulus Congestus Clouds

These are impressive, hard-to-ignore clouds that tower high in the sky with solid-looking, cauliflower-like towers. Some of these clouds grow into fierce thunderstorms.

KEY FACTS

Cumulus congestus clouds are also called "towering cumulus" because they are usually taller than wide.

+ fact: Congestus clouds can produce heavy and prolonged rain or snow showers without growing into cumulonimbus clouds.

+ fact: Cumulus congestus clouds can form as individual clouds or as a wall of clouds.

Cumulus congestus clouds form on days when the atmosphere up to great heights is unstable. Thermals of warm air begin rising from the ground at about 50 mph (80 kph) or faster. As the rising air cools, water vapor begins condensing into tiny cloud drops. The cauliflower-like parts of the cloud are made of tiny water drops that reflect more light than the softer, fibrous parts of the cloud, which are made of ice crystals. When parts of the cloud begin to take on the softer look, it shows the cloud is "glaciating"—ice crystals are forming, which is the beginning of its transformation into a cumulonimbus or thunderstorm.

Cumulonimbus Clouds

A cumulonimbus, commonly called a thunderstorm, is the only cloud requiring caution when nearby. Its potential dangers include lightning, tornadoes, and dangerous straight-line winds.

KEY FACTS

Thunderstorm tops are typically 20,000 ft (6,100 m) above the ground and at times 75,000 ft (23,000 m) high.

+ fact: Cumulonimbus clouds usually reach their peak strength in late afternoon.

+ fact: Thunderstorms occur as individual storms, in large and small clusters, and in lines 200 mi (300 km) or more long.

Meteorologists consider a cumulus congestus to have become a cumulonimbus when at least the top part of the cloud has taken on the smooth, fibrous, glaciated appearance that comes when this part of the cloud is mostly ice. A sure sign is that the top of the cloud begins to flatten out into a characteristic anvil shape. Thunderstorm precipitation is showery. It starts and stops suddenly, and it can be quite heavy over a relatively small area while nearby areas are dry. The general winds in an area push thunderstorms across the countryside, as they do other clouds, sometimes as fast at 50 mph (80 kph) but usually more slowly. Thunderstorms are quite turbulent inside the cloud.

Pyrocumulus Clouds

Pyrocumulus or "fire cumulus" clouds form over large fires, usually wildfires, under certain atmospheric conditions. They can threaten wildfire-fighters with hard-to-forecast wind shifts.

KEY FACTS

Fires sometimes create tornado-like "fire whirls"; most last a few minutes but some persist for 20 minutes and spread the fire.

+ fact: Pyrocumulus clouds sometimes grow into thunderstorms—pyrocumulonimbus.

+ fact: Volcanic eruptions create pyrocumulus clouds. The mushroom cloud of a nuclear bomb is a pyrocumulus.

Wildfires are dangerous enough, but if they burn during days when the atmosphere is unstable and dry with light upper air winds, they become especially dangerous for firefighters. Under those conditions, a fire's hot air will rise straight up, 20,000 feet (6,100 m) and more, to create a pyrocumulus cloud. Air rushing in from around the fire to replace the rising air fans the flames. These winds can also change direction with little warning, especially on mountains and in hills, sending fire in new directions and potentially trapping firefighters. While the bottom of a pyrocumulus might be brown or gray with smoke, the top is bright white, like the tops of other cumulus clouds. Pyrocumulus clouds don't have enough water to produce the rain that would put out a fire.

Billow Clouds

The lovely wave formations atop billow clouds are spawned by forces that are common in the atmosphere and create other phenomena, such as ocean waves.

KEY FACTS

Lord Kelvin, a Scottish physicist, and Hermann von Helmholtz, a German scientist, mathematically analyzed waves in the 19th century.

+ fact: Waves form at the boundary between fluids with different densities.

+ fact: The distance between each cloud wave is usually between 3,200 and 6,500 ft (1,000 and 2,000 m).

Billow clouds, also called Kelvin-Helmholtz clouds or waves, usually occur at a layer of warm air high above the ground. Up there, with the warm air above and cold air below, winds are blowing in opposing directions, and the curving pattern develops. To envision what happens, imagine holding a ball between the palms of your hands and moving your hands back and forth in opposite directions. To form billow clouds, the air rolls between two outside layers of air moving in opposite directions, just like the ball rolls between your hands. The rolling air might not complete the circle, though, creating forms that look like breaking ocean waves.

Supercell Thunderstorm Clouds

Supercells are the most dangerous but the least common thunderstorms. They produce almost all of the deadliest tornadoes. Distinct features make supercells stand out.

KEY FACTS

Haze and hills in the U.S. Southeast and East often make it difficult to see enough of a thunderstorm to determine if it is a supercell.

+ fact: Strong supercells have a dome on the top, called an "overshooting top."

+ fact: Low-precipitation supercells on the arid High Plains produce little rain or hail.

A supercell is a long-lasting kind of thunderstorm that produces strong tornadoes and other dangerous weather. A mesocyclone—a one- to 10-mile-wide rotating updraft that carries air from the ground to the storm's top—distinguishes supercells from all other thunderstorms. You can often see its barber-pole striations. Supercells develop a wall cloud between the area of precipitation from the thunderstorm and a precipitation-free base. The wall cloud forms where wet, cool air is being drawn into the thunderstorm's updraft. A wall cloud that lasts more than ten minutes and moves violently is most likely to produce a tornado.

Shelf and Roll Clouds

Shelf and roll clouds form on top of air that descended in a thunderstorm and moves away from the storm. A shelf cloud is attached to its parent thunderstorm; a roll cloud has broken away.

Air descending from a thunderstorm travels away from the storm, becoming a dome of cool air that is called a gust front. As its leading edge meets and plows into warm, humid air, it pushes the air up. The warm air cools, and its humidity condenses to form a shelf cloud atop the cool downdraft air. Such a gust front can last more than a day and travel hundreds of miles to help trigger new thunderstorms by pushing up warm, humid air. If the front of the shelf cloud is ragged, pushing rising, small, ragged clouds in front of it, damaging wind squalls and shifts in wind direction will likely result.

|||||||||||||||||||||||||||||||||||||||||||||||||||||||||||||||||||||||||||||||||||||

Dew

Dew, the water that you often find on the grass and your car on some early mornings, is one of the many ways water moves out of and back into the atmosphere.

KEY FACTS

The term "dew point" refers to the temperature at which condensation begins on the ground or in the air.

+ fact: Dew on grass mostly evaporated from the grass and stayed in the air nearby until condensing back onto the grass.

+ fact: Dew often forms first on car roofs because they radiate heat directly away.

D ew begins condensing when the air cools to the dew point—a temperature point that varies depending on how much water vapor is in the air. Because warm air can hold more water than cold air, water vapor will begin condensing from very humid air at a higher temperature than it would condense from air with very little water vapor. Dew begins forming on grass and other low-lying plants, because air sinks as it cools and air along the ground is usually colder than air just a little higher up. Calm, clear, still nights encourage dew. These are nights without wind that mixes the air, and with heat radiating directly to space. You can't rely on the old folklore that says a dewy morning means the day will be clear, because a new weather system can move in with clouds and rain.

Frost

Frost forms when water vapor in the air becomes ice without first condensing into water through a process called deposition. It forms on clear, calm nights with temperatures below 32°F (0°C).

KEY FACTS

Frost can form on the ground when the official temperature—measured above ground level—is above freezing.

+ fact: "Black frost" occurs when frigid air kills plants without visible frost.

+ fact: The growing season runs from the average date of spring's last frost to the average date of fall's first frost.

Frost forms overnight as white crystals on grass and other objects. With enough humidity in the air, these begin growing new crystals, which are called hoarfrost. Snowbanks are a good place to look for hoarfrost because some of the snow sublimates directly into water vapor during the day, and the vapor stays near the snow on calm days. At night, the vapor deposits into hoarfrost crystals, which cause the snow to sparkle. Frost forms on the inside of windowpanes that are not well insulated when it is moderately humid inside and very cold outside. Imperfections or scratches help shape the patterns that form. Frost can form on double-pane windows.

Rain

Clouds are made of water in the atmosphere, but they do not always cause precipitation. All rain falls from clouds, but most clouds do not produce rain.

KEY FACTS

Meteorologists have agreed on standard descriptions of rain.

+ fact: Light rain falls at up to 0.10 in (2.54 mm) an hour; scattered drops are seen.

+ fact: Moderate rain falls from 0.11–0.30 in (2.79–7.62 mm) an hour; drops aren't clearly seen.

+ fact: Heavy rain falls at more than 0.30 in an hour in sheets.

A freezing cold rain and a warm rain both involve precipitation, but clouds that are colder than 32°F (0°C) and those that are warmer produce rain in different ways. In both, roughly a million cloud drops come together to produce a raindrop 0.08 inch (2 mm) in size. But in warm clouds, a few slightly enlarged cloud drops fall and sweep up others to grow into raindrops. In freezing cold, when ice and water mix, water vapor migrates into ice crystals that grow heavy enough to fall. If the air below is warmer, the ice crystals melt into rain; if not, they come down as freezing rain. See shapes of small and large drops at right.

Drizzle

Drizzle consists of water drops less than 0.02 inches (0.5 mm) in diameter. Ordinary drizzle causes few problems to everyday life, but freezing drizzle turns to ice on impact and can pose a danger.

KEY FACTS

Visibility determines drizzle's intensity. More than a half mile (0.8 km) is light; between a quarter (0.4 km) and a half mile is moderate; less than a quarter mile is heavy.

+ fact: Drizzle drops fall close together and float in air currents.

+ fact: Drizzle is most likely in November and least likely in July in North America.

Drizzle falls mostly from stratiform or stratocumulus clouds. Climate scientists are especially interested in the drizzle from the shallow stratocumulus clouds that cover large areas of subtropical oceans—the areas just north and south of the tropics. These clouds are important for cooling the Earth, and researchers are investigating the role oceanic drizzle plays on these clouds and their effects. For most of us, drizzle means nothing more than a gloomy day—except for the ice that freezing drizzle leaves on roads and sidewalks. Drizzle-size drops that freeze on impact are especially dangerous for aircraft encountering them in the clouds or as they fall. Drizzle helps illustrate how even tiny atmospheric phenomena can be important.

Sleet

Sleet generally refers to frozen raindrops less than 0.2 inch (5 mm) in diameter that fall during winter storms often with, before, or after freezing rain and snow.

KEY FACTS

The eastern United States and southeastern Canada are the only places where sleet accumulates to a thickness of more than 0.8 in (20 mm).

+ fact: The U.S. National Weather Service issues a "sleet warning" when more than a half inch (12.7 mm) is expected.

+ fact: Sleet bounces and can be heard when it hits.

Sleet forms when a layer of air above freezing temperature (32°F; 0°C) lies 5,000–10,000 feet (1,500–3,000 m) above the ground, sandwiched between layers of colder, below-freezing air above and below. Snow falls from the higher layer of cold air into the middle layer of warm air. It melts, falls into the lower layer of cold air, and refreezes into ice pellets. These pellets can be spherical, conical, or irregular in shape. In North America, sleet can mount up to as high as 2 inches (5 cm). Such accumulations occur when a strong storm pushes warm air over a layer of dense, cold air at the surface for a few hundred miles. Sleet likely comes ahead of an advancing warm front.

Freezing Rain

Freezing rain occurs when raindrops that are supercooled—cooled to below 32°F (0°C) but not frozen—instantly turn into ice when they hit cold objects such as roads and power lines.

KEY FACTS

Warm fronts bring freezing rain as a layer of warm air moves over ground-level frigid air.

+ fact: Freezing rain causes black ice: a slick, transparent layer of solid ice atop a flat surface such as a road.

+ fact: Some estimate that as many as one-fourth of winter accidents are caused by freezing rain.

As with sleet, layers of warmer air sandwiched between layers of cold air during winter storms set the stage for freezing rain. In some circumstances, the layer of below-freezing air at ground level isn't thick enough to freeze raindrops into sleet. Then the drops become supercooled and coat everything cold that they hit with a heavy glaze of solid ice. The weight of this clinging ice can bring down tree limbs and power lines. Plows have a harder time clearing ice from roads than snow. The ice is slicker than snow, causing more cars to spin out or slide off roads. When freezing rain is forecast, road crews often spray chemicals such as calcium magnesium acetate on pavement. The chemicals inhibit ice from forming or keep ice that does form from sticking to roads.

Snow

Snow is frozen precipitation that forms as six-sided crystals by the direct deposition of water vapor as ice on freezing nuclei or on tiny ice crystals in clouds.

KEY FACTS

Visibility determines snowfall intensity: More than a half mile (0.8 km) is light, between a quarter (0.4 km) and a half mile is moderate, less than a quarter mile is heavy.

+ fact: Snow flurries are light showers with little accumulation.

+ fact: Blizzards are heavy snowfalls lasting 3 hours or more with winds of 35 mph (56 kph) or faster.

Temperature and humidity determine the shape of snow crystals. They may start as six-sided crystals, but they often reach the ground in more simple or more complex forms, depending on the conditions they encounter as they fall. When supercooled water drops hit a snow crystal, they stick to it as rime, a coating of ice. This process can create snow pellets—spherical white particles up to 0.2 inch (5 mm) across. In near-freezing temperatures, crystals stick together to form snowflakes, sometimes large agglomerations. If you closely examine snow, you might see various forms of hexagonal snow crystals as well as indistinct pieces of ice broken off from crystals. Snow that falls in air close to freezing is heavier than snow in colder air.

Snow Crystals

When water cools to 32°F (0°C), its molecules align themselves as six-sided ice crystals. When these crystals grow in the air, they retain a hexagonal shape but assume shapes of infinite variety.

KEY FACTS

The shape of snow crystals has long fascinated scientists.

+ fact: In 1611, Johannes Kepler wrote that snow crystals have six sides.

+ fact: In 1665, Robert Hooke sketched ice crystals he saw through a microscope.

+ fact: In the 1930s, Ukichiro Nakaya found that temperature and humidity determine crystal shapes.

If you collect and examine snowflakes as they fall—a dark piece of cardboard works, or even a dark-colored sleeve—you'll discover few like the lacy dendritic (branching) snowflake designs created for winter-season decorations. In fact, you're more likely to see broken bits of crystal shapes that tumbled against one another as they fell. If you don't see crystals with regular shapes the first time you try, don't give up. Eventually you should happen to collect crystals that are more than broken pieces. You could find that observing snow crystals, as with other aspects of weather, can take you deep into physics and other physical sciences.

Thunderstorms

Cumulus clouds grow and proceed through predictable stages as they turn into thunderstorms. Learning about thunderstorm stages is a first step toward understanding them.

KEY FACTS

A thunderstorm's life cycle has three stages.

+ fact: First is a towering cumulus stage as rising air forms a growing cloud.

+ fact: The mature stage, the longest, begins when rain starts falling, dragging down cold air.

+ fact: The dissipating stage begins when updrafts end, leaving only downdrafts until the storm dies.

As an ordinary cumulus cloud grows into a cumulus congestus and then a cumulonimbus, surging updrafts rise to form the cauliflower-like thunderstorm clouds. Water vapor becomes cloud drops, which grow into raindrops. When parts of the cloud become smooth, ice crystals are forming. This process of glaciation releases more energy and generates more updraft, which can help spur the formation of the telltale anvil shape at the top of a thunderstorm cloud. In the mature stage, updrafts can be faster than 100 mph (160 kph); accompanying downdrafts measure half that speed. In fierce thunderstorms, especially supercells, a storm's mature stage can last for hours. Rain will not begin to die off until updrafts stop feeding the cloud.

||||||||||||||||||||||||||||||||||||||||||||||||||||||||||||||||||||||||||||||||||||||||||||||||

Multicell Cluster Thunderstorms

A large cumulonimbus cloud that is producing lightning with more than one dome on top, maybe an anvil on one side, is a multicell cluster of thunderstorms.

KEY FACTS

Multicell cluster thunderstorms line up in the direction the winds are blowing.

+ fact: New cells usually form at the side from which the wind is blowing; cells mature in the cluster's center.

+ fact: Each cell of a cluster lasts approximately 20 minutes, but the cluster itself can keep going for hours.

Although many thunderstorms go though three distinct stages as separate, single-cell storms, groups of related storms either in clusters or lines are more common. A multicell cluster forms when the downdrafts from one thunderstorm push air up to trigger an adjacent thunderstorm. This storm in turn can trigger a new one as the original storm is dissipating. A cluster will often have at least one storm in the dissipating stage, one mature storm, and one still in the towering cumulus stage, with the clouds of all of them blending. The wind pushes thunderstorms in a cluster in the same direction.

Mature stage   Dissipating stage

Towering Cumulus

Supercells

These thunderstorms are "super" in terms of their size, how long they last, and their potential for causing death and destruction. Supercells produce almost all of the most deadly tornadoes.

KEY FACTS

A supercell can last for several hours, even when it is producing tornadoes along the way.

+ fact: Tops of Great Plains supercells reach 40,000 ft (12,000 m) above the ground.

+ fact: Landforms influence the size and life span of supercells. Those occurring in the eastern U.S. are generally smaller than those on the Great Plains.

Although most single-cell thunderstorms last less than a half hour, supercells can last for hours. Winds from different directions at various altitudes cause the main updraft to lean instead of traveling straight up and down, which means that rain falling from the top of the storm doesn't cool the cloud's rising warm air, and so the updraft keeps going. Many supercells produce only weak tornadoes, but some can be deadly. Researchers are looking for ways to distinguish well in advance which supercells will be the most dangerous and which will bring no major threats. When you see a supercell, you should stay alert for a tornado.

Squall Line Thunderstorms

If you see a long line of approaching thunderstorms preceded by a shelf cloud—a low-hanging, horizontal, wedge-shaped cloud—prepare for strong winds and lightning.

KEY FACTS

A squall line can stretch for hundreds of miles—as far as from Louisiana into Illinois. Airliners detouring around them can cause major delays.

+ fact: Squall line thunderstorms line up at roughly a right angle to the wind direction.

+ fact: Most squall lines last from late morning or early afternoon until after dark.

Steady winds can push a line of thunderstorms together in the same direction. The advancing storms scoop up warm, humid air, which feeds the storms even further. As individual storms die, new ones take their place in the line. Tornadoes sometimes occur, but a squall line's major danger is fierce straight-line winds that blast down in the direction the storms are moving. Individual storms in a line can reach more than 40,000 feet (12,000 m) into the air, too high for airliners to fly over. Squall lines can occur right along cold fronts, but the strongest are usually those several miles ahead of a cold front.

Upper air winds

Derecho

A derecho is an extremely long-lasting, fast-moving thunderstorm squall line that produces winds of at least 57 mph (92 kph) along a path at least 240 miles (386 km) long.

KEY FACTS

The term "derecho" was first used by Gustavus Hinrichs, a University of Iowa professor, in an 1888 scientific journal article.

+ fact: Hinrichs chose *derecho,* Spanish for "straight ahead," to distinguish its straight-line winds from a tornado's rotating winds.

+ fact: The National Weather Service began using "derecho" in 1987.

In the late spring and early summer, especially strong, long-lasting squall lines called derechos move across the Great Plains from the Rocky Mountains and sometimes all the way to the Atlantic coast. As in any squall line, the individual thunderstorms making up a derecho weaken and die, soon replaced by new ones, and so the damage along a derecho's path is not consistent. Winds build up to extreme speeds because the downburst force from individual thunderstorms is added to the speed of the wind pushing the squall line to the east. A derecho dies when it runs into dry air in the upper atmosphere or when the winds pushing it die down. Most derechos occur in the summer, most likely during heat waves, and mostly east of the Rocky Mountains.

Bow Echoes

A bow echo storm is an especially dangerous curved line of thunderstorms. The most dangerous winds occur at the crest or center of the curving bow-shaped formation of clouds.

KEY FACTS

A bow echo can range in size from 12 to 125 mi (20 to 200 km) across and last from 3 to 6 hours.

+ fact: Tornadoes often form on each end of a bow echo, but these are usually weak, doing little damage.

+ fact: On November 2, 1995, a bow echo hit the Hawaiian island of Kauai with winds of 90 mph (145 kph).

At times, winds blast down from part of a squall line or an isolated supercell and race ahead of the line or the supercell right above the ground. This soft, fast-moving wind, called a rear-inflow jet, pushes warm, humid air up and triggers a line of thunderstorms that form in a bow shape. T. Theodore Fujita, the famed 20th-century Japanese-American tornado researcher, discovered and named bow echo damage patterns and radar images while investigating a derecho that struck from Michigan to Minnesota on July 4, 1977. Almost all derechos produce bow echoes, which often cause the derecho's most destructive winds.

Mesoscale Convective Complex

A mesoscale convective complex (MCC) is experienced as a long summer night with constant thunderstorm downpours and frequent lightning, usually on the Great Plains.

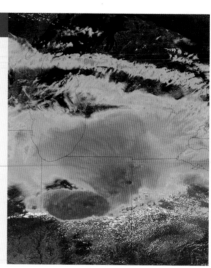

KEY FACTS

Each word in "mesoscale convective complex" describes an element of this storm.

+ fact: Mesoscale: midsize weather phenomena, from a few miles to a few hundred miles across

+ fact: Convective: movement of air up and down

+ fact: Complex: storms are interrelated, not just happening to be together

By definition, a mesoscale convective complex (MCC) is a persistent, nearly circular area of clouds measuring a temperature of -25°F (-32°C). Generally thunderstorm anvils, they cover a huge area—at least 38,500 square miles (99,700 sq km), roughly the size of Iowa. The system begins in the late afternoon and early evening with heavy rain and sometimes strong winds. By early morning, the thunderstorms die and the complex's rotating vortex, taller than 10,000 feet (3,000 m), continues traveling to the east. It can reignite the MCC the next evening. Meteorologists didn't realize MCCs were organized systems until weather satellite images showing cloud-top temperatures, thus their heights, became available in the 1970s. MCCs mostly affect the middle of the U.S.

Lightning

Lightning is a huge electrical spark flashing between areas of opposite electrical charge. It occurs inside clouds, from a cloud to the ground, from a cloud to another cloud, or into empty air.

KEY FACTS

Separate current strokes lasting a few tenths of a second cause the flickering lightning flash you see.

+ fact: Lightning's rapid heating and cooling of the air creates the sound waves we hear as thunder.

+ fact: Thunder rumbles as sounds from different parts of the flash arrive at slightly different times.

The violent churning of mixed ice crystals and water drops within a thunderstorm leaves areas of negative and positive charge in different parts of a cloud, usually with a strong negative charge near the cloud's bottom. Attraction between this and positive charge on the ground causes streams of negative charge to begin working their way down through the air as stepped leaders that zig one way, zag another. These create paths for stronger currents. When one of these connects with something on the ground, such as a tree or a lightning rod, a strong return stroke, which we see as lightning, flashes from the ground to the cloud.

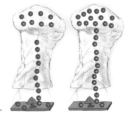

Lightning to Worry About

About 100,000 thunderstorms occur in the United States each year, according to the National Weather Service. Lightning makes each one dangerous, no matter how weak it is.

KEY FACTS

A flash of lightning measures approximately 50,000°F (27,760°C), but it lasts so briefly that a victim does not suffer deep burns.

+ fact: Lightning can cause random neurological damage or stop a victim's heart.

+ fact: Lightning rods, which carry lightning into the ground, have changed little since Benjamin Franklin's invention.

Most lightning flashes are a negative charge attracted to the ground's strong positive charge. To avoid lightning damage, you need to provide lightning a low-resistance path to the ground such as a lightning rod kept in good condition with no breaks in its path into the ground. To prevent injury or death by a lightning strike outside, stay away from lightning's path to the ground by being inside a sturdy building or a hardtop vehicle. Because lightning goes into the ground, it can hit and damage underground utility lines. Water pipes can give lightning a path inside your home. Indoors during a thunderstorm you shouldn't be near plugged-in appliances or computers, take a shower or bath, or talk on a phone with a cord. Cordless and cell phones are safe to use indoors during a thunderstorm.

Upper Atmospheric Lightning

A few thunderstorms put on stunning but hard-to-see shows of phenomena called sprites, elves, and blue jets above the storms as lightning flashes in and below the clouds.

Going back to at least World War II, airplane pilots reported unusual lights above thunderstorms, causing scientists to wonder what meteorological activity happens above as well as below thunderstorms. It was not until 1989 that scientists testing a low-light video saw the first images of a sprite, a large discharge of energy above a thunderstorm. Unless you're an airline pilot, you will have to make a special effort to see these upper atmospheric lightning phenomena. The best way to try to observe them is to be somewhere high, such as the Rocky Mountain Front Range. Choose a clear night and pick a location that is far from city lights. Wait until your eyes become adapted to the darkness, and then look out over the tops of distant thunderstorms on the Great Plains.

When Lightning Hits Airplanes

On average, lightning hits each airliner flying over North America once a year, but today's aircraft are built to shrug off the charge. Lightning last caused a U.S. airline crash in 1962.

KEY FACTS

Lightning frequently hits aircraft today.

+ fact: Airplanes and rockets can trigger lightning by flying into strong electrical fields.

+ fact: Lightning hit NASA's lightning research plane 714 times.

+ fact: Lightning-struck just 26.5 seconds after blastoff in 1969, Apollo 12 forged on to make the second manned moon landing.

When lightning hits an airplane, the electricity spreads out and flows through the aluminum skin and then back out into the air. The only damage caused includes small burn marks where the lightning entered and left the airplane. Fuel tanks have extra metal around them to keep lightning hits from burning through. Shielding protects electrical systems from the direct flow of lightning currents and from currents lightning can induce in wires. Advanced composite aircraft such as Boeing's 787 Dreamliner have conductive material embedded in the skin. Even if lightning hits, no one aboard a commercial aircraft today is in danger of being shocked. Lightning's threat to those servicing airplanes on the ground can delay flights.

Saint Elmo's Fire

Strong electrical fields rip electrons from nitrogen and oxygen molecules in the air causing a harmless blue-violet glow called Saint Elmo's fire, usually on tapered objects.

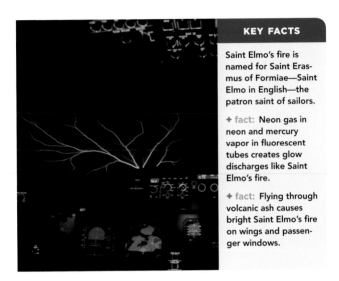

KEY FACTS

Saint Elmo's fire is named for Saint Erasmus of Formiae—Saint Elmo in English—the patron saint of sailors.

+ fact: Neon gas in neon and mercury vapor in fluorescent tubes creates glow discharges like Saint Elmo's fire.

+ fact: Flying through volcanic ash causes bright Saint Elmo's fire on wings and passenger windows.

Saint Elmo's fire is a natural blue-violet glow caused by a strong electrical field tearing apart the air's molecules of nitrogen and oxygen—a process called ionization. The resulting Saint Elmo's fire is a plasma. Curves and sharp points concentrate electronic fields, making the glow stronger. In past centuries, people saw Saint Elmo's fire at the top of ship masts and church steeples. The glow seemed miraculous because, though it looks like fire, it produces no heat and does not burn ships' wooden masts. Today, you are most likely to see Saint Elmo's fire on the tips of airplane wings. Pilots regularly see it around their windshields. In 1749 Benjamin Franklin became the first scientist to describe Saint Elmo's fire as an atmospheric electrical phenomenon. He sometimes saw it on the tips of lightning rods before lightning hit the rods.

Ball Lightning

Since the time of the ancient Greeks and Romans, people have reported glowing, floating balls in the air, associating them with lightning, yet scientists are still unable to explain what's going on.

KEY FACTS

Most reports of ball lightning indicate that it is harmless. Scientists can't explain it.

+ fact: Ball lightning is roughly the size of a grapefruit and as bright as a 60-watt bulb.

+ fact: Laboratory experiments have created objects with aspects of ball lightning, but have not entirely matched reports of it.

This unusual phenomenon is called ball lightning because it often resembles a floating ball. Almost everyone who has viewed a ball says it appeared either just after a lightning strike or when lightning was striking nearby. Researchers have compiled at least 10,000 reports of ball lightning in recent decades. Some observers report ball lightning passing through windows without causing damage; others report seeing it appear and disappear inside airplanes in flight, again with no damage. Mysteriously, it glows without giving off heat and does not appear to generate power. Individuals and groups of people have reported ball lightning since the time of ancient Greece. Glowing balls approximately six inches (15 cm) in diameter floating in the air have persuaded many scientists that ball lightning is real.

Hail

Hailstones are pieces of ice that form in thunderstorm updrafts, which keep them from falling while more water freezes onto them. Updraft speed determines the size of hailstones.

KEY FACTS

A hailstone 1 inch (2.5 cm) in diameter needs a 20 mph (32 kph) updraft to form; a 0.75-inch (1.9 cm) stone needs a 64 mph (103 kph) updraft.

+ fact: More hail falls yearly on northeastern Colorado and southeastern Wyoming than elsewhere in the U.S.

+ fact: The National Oceanic and Atmospheric Administration says hail injures 24 people in the U.S. each year; deaths are very rare.

Most hailstones form in multicell, supercell, or cold-front squall line thunderstorms, usually near the center of a storm. Hail begins forming as tiny ice pellets collide with supercooled water droplets that freeze on contact with the ice. As they grow, hailstones may make several up-and-down trips within the center of the storm before the updraft weakens or they become heavy enough to fall. By definition, a thunderstorm that produces 1-inch (19 mm) hail is severe because of the strong updrafts and other winds in the system. Very strong updrafts can carry hailstones high into a storm and then sweep to one side, so that they fall outside the storm itself.

Microbursts

A microburst is an intense, concentrated wind that blasts down from a shower or thunderstorm, affecting an area no longer than 2.5 miles (4 km) on a side with strong, gusty winds.

KEY FACTS

Wind damage often shows whether a microburst or a tornado caused it.

+ fact: The National Weather Service has 48 Terminal Doppler Weather Radars to detect airport microbursts.

+ fact: In 1983, a 138 mph (222 kph) microburst hit Andrews Air Force Base three minutes after *Air Force One* carrying President Ronald Reagan landed.

Microbursts can blow down big trees, so people should avoid standing near trees during a windy thunderstorm. The greater danger of microbursts is to flying aircraft. Meteorologists did not have a name for microbursts until the 1970s, when researcher T. Theodore Fujita coined the term "microburst" to describe the concentrated winds that had caused several airplane crashes. Once the term was in use, pilots and air traffic controllers were better able to observe and avoid them. Through 1985, the U.S. air industry suffered roughly one fatal microburst airliner crash every 18 months, but since then, only one has occurred, thanks to better warnings.

|||||||||||||||||||||||||||||||||||||||||||||||||||||||||||||||||||||||||||||||

Gust Front

Air coming down from a thunderstorm moves over the ground as a miniature cold front, or gust front. Effects include bringing slightly cooler temperatures and triggering new thunderstorms.

KEY FACTS

You may feel a distant thunderstorm's gust front as a cool breeze on a hot day.

+ fact: Outflow boundaries, or gust fronts, interacting with supercell thunderstorms increase the odds that the supercell will produce tornadoes.

+ fact: A gust front hitting an airport can endanger takeoffs and landings with unexpected wind shifts.

Meteorologists call gust fronts "outflow boundaries" because they do more than bring a quick shot of refreshing cool air. They can travel long distances and persist longer than 24 hours with small temperature differences in the air across the front. Even small changes can help trigger new thunderstorms and affect existing storms. Streams of air converge along gust fronts, bringing dust, insects, and other small objects that Doppler radar can see long after the gust front forms.

Meteorologists use such gust front images to forecast where new thunderstorms are likely to begin. For instance, the meeting point of two gust fronts, each of which may be a day old, is a prime location for where storms may be expected to originate and then develop.

Funnel Cloud

A funnel-shaped cloud full of condensed water stretching down from a towering cumulus cloud or cumulonimbus might be called a tornado that is not touching the ground.

KEY FACTS

When the air is too dry for a condensation funnel to form, the first sign of a tornado can be spinning debris on the ground.

+ fact: A tornado's spinning winds extend wider than the visible funnel.

+ fact: Funnels turn from white to black or other colors when they pick up dirt or dust from the ground.

A funnel dipping down out of a storm cloud is a funnel cloud as long as it neither touches the ground nor kicks up dust or debris from the ground. Once either of those conditions occurs, it has become a tornado. This type of condensation funnel forms when falling atmospheric pressure in the vortex, or spinning funnel, cools the air enough for water vapor to condense into a swirling cloud. They often burn out of energy within a few minutes. Almost all tornadoes begin as funnel clouds, but many funnel clouds never become tornadoes. Meteorologists sometimes talk of cold air funnels: They don't form in thunderstorms, they are generally weak, and they don't last long, although a few might touch down briefly as weak tornadoes or waterspouts.

Tornadoes

Tornadoes are rotating columns of air hanging from a cumulonimbus or sometimes a cumulus congestus cloud that have grown long enough to come in contact with the ground.

KEY FACTS

Tornadoes are ranked on the Enhanced Fujita Scale.

+ fact: Weak: F0, 65–85 mph (105–137 kph); F1, 86–110 mph (138–177 kph)

+ fact: Strong: F2, 111–135 mph (179–218 kph); F3, 135–165 mph (219–266 kph)

+ fact: Violent: F4, 166–200 mph (267–322 kph); F5, faster than 200 mph (322 kph)

The wind speed of tornadoes can range from 40 mph (64 kph) to more than 300 mph (483 kph). Tornadoes are the most destructive of all local weather phenomena. Because strong tornadoes destroy wind instruments, the Fujita scale measures storms by the damage caused. Those ranked F4 or above account for more than 70 percent of all tornado deaths and the greatest destruction. Fortunately, about three-fourths of all tornadoes are weaker, with winds no faster than 110 mph (177 kph). The United States averages more than 1,000 tornadoes a year, more than any other nation; Canada ranks second.

Multiple Vortex Tornadoes

Many tornadoes, especially the larger ones, are packages of twisters with smaller vortices circling around the central tornado's perimeter, sometimes seen but often hidden.

KEY FACTS

Three seems the most common number of subvortices in multiple vortex tornadoes, but spotters have seen as many as seven.

+ fact: Some hurricane eyewalls have small vortices that look and act like tornado subvortices.

+ fact: Spotters reported multiple vortices before the May 22, 2011, tornado hit Joplin, Missouri, killing 161 people.

Why does it happen that a tornado can destroy a well-built house while a similar house, right next door, escapes with minor damage? The existence of multiple vortex tornadoes explains this phenomenon. The heavy damage occurs where the winds of the main tornado combine with the winds of a subvortex moving in the same direction, thus multiplying the impact. At times, this combination of forces can add 100 mph (160 kph) to the wind, spotlighting small areas in the tornado's larger path. Tornado spotters most likely see multiple vortices as a tornado is beginning, before dust and debris darken the main funnel. Damage patterns can confirm the vortices.

Waterspouts

A common definition of a waterspout is "a tornado over water," but meteorologists prefer to use the term for weak, non-supercell vortices that form below cumulus congestus clouds.

KEY FACTS

A waterspout's con-densation funnel is not water sucked up from below; it is condensed from water vapor in the air above.

+ fact: A waterspout's life cycle is usually less than 20 minutes; winds reach speeds no greater than 85 mph (137 kph).

+ fact: A fall water-spout season often occurs on the Great Lakes.

Waterspouts most often form from the bottoms of dark, growing cumulus clouds. The first sign of a waterspout forming is a dark spot on the water's surface where the still invisible funnel has touched down; it may be kicking up water spray as well. Many waterspouts die out in this early stage, but sometimes they develop to the stage that a condensation funnel is visible, coming down from the cloud to the dark spot. The oceans around southern Florida, especially in the Keys, have more water-spouts than any other part of the United States. Non-supercell waterspouts are generally weak, which means that they aren't as dangerous as most ordinary tornadoes, but boaters should not ignore them. Waterspouts can be stronger than they appear.

Dust Devils

A dust devil is a small whirlwind that, unlike a tornado, is not attached to a cloud. Dust devils usually occur in hot, dry locations where dust or sand makes them visible.

KEY FACTS

The strongest dust devils occur in the hottest deserts, but small ones can occasionally occur in cities as well.

+ fact: Dust devil winds sometimes build to the speed of an F1 tornado, up to 110 mph (177 kph).

+ fact: The Viking orbiters NASA sent to Mars in the 1970s discovered that dust devils occur on the red planet.

Dust devils form in thermals of rising air and often develop a funnel-like shape as air flows out of the top. The air cools as it rises and then eventually sinks back to the ground, where it can create the light breezes that spin thermals into dust devils. Dust devils can develop to a height of 3,000 feet (1,000 m) or more on some of the hottest deserts. They are usually benign, but they occasionally cause damage and injuries. On September 14, 2000, for example, a dust devil hit the Coconino County Fairgrounds in Flagstaff, Arizona, causing minor injuries and damaging booths and tents.

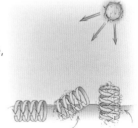

Acid Rain

Acid rain describes precipitation made slightly acidic by air pollution, often from far away. It wreaks damage on both the natural environment and on limestone and marble buildings.

KEY FACTS

Acid rain's most damaging effects occur in locations where the soils do not naturally neutralize acids.

+ fact: Acid rain leaches calcium from soil, depriving plants of an important nutrient.

+ fact: Robert Angus Smith, a Scottish chemist, coined the term "acid rain" in 1852 and linked it to damage it causes.

Although the phenomenon likely dates back a century or two, only in the mid-20th century did people begin to take responsibility for acid rain and its consequences. Most acid rain in North America develops from sulfur dioxide and nitrogen oxides produced by burning fossil fuels, mostly to generate electricity and run cars and trucks. The acid rain does not come directly from smokestacks or tailpipes. Instead, the emissions react with water in the atmosphere to create damaging compounds that can travel hundreds of miles from their sources. The pollutants can fall as dry materials as well as in rain or snow. The chemicals make soil, rivers, lakes, and ponds slightly acidic, potentially killing smaller animals and plants. Air quality rules are reducing acid rain, and some hard-hit areas in the Northeast are recovering.

Hurricanes

A hurricane is a tropical cyclone in the Atlantic, the eastern Pacific, the Caribbean Sea, or the Gulf of Mexico—in which winds reach a sustained speed of 74 mph (119 kph) for a minute or more.

KEY FACTS

A tropical cyclone becomes a tropical storm when its winds reach 39 mph (63 kph), at which time it is assigned a name from a pre-selected list.

+ fact: Sustained winds of 74 mph (119 kph) make it a hurricane.

+ fact: Hurricanes are classified on a scale from 1 to 5 in order of severity based on wind speed.

Tropical cyclones are born over ocean water that is warmer than 80°F (27°C) and in a condition of high humidity. Because they draw their energy from warm water, these storms weaken and die when they move over cool water or land. A mature hurricane system rotates counterclockwise with a diameter of hundreds of miles and an eye of mostly clear air and light winds in the center.

The fastest winds are usually in the eyewall—the ring of thunderstorms encircling the eye. Rain bands of thunderstorms spiral around the storm and into the eyewall. A hurricane pushes water ahead, creating a storm surge when it comes ashore.

Steering current

Air leaving the storm's top

Low-level winds spiraling into the storm

Hurricane Forecasting

Radar, satellites, sea buoys, and reconnaissance flights contribute to improved methods of hurricane forecasting, so that meteorologists can often predict a hurricane's path a week ahead.

Hurricane forecasts are fast improving, but they are still far from perfect. From 1970 to 2012, the average error in track forecasts for three days into the future shrank from 518 miles to 138 miles (834 to 222 km). That is a significant improvement, but it means that if a strong hurricane is forecast to hit in three days, anyone located 200 miles (322 km) on each side of the forecast strike zone should be alert for changes in the forecast and ready to evacuate. Forecasters also assess climate variables to predict the number of hurricanes in a given season, still an inexact science as well.

Extratropical Cyclones

In brief, these are large storm systems that form over cold air or cold water away from the tropics. They account for almost all stormy weather in the middle and polar latitudes all year.

KEY FACTS

Fronts are defined by the interaction of air masses at their boundaries.

+ fact: At a cold front relatively cold air is advancing to replace warmer air.

+ fact: At a warm front relatively warm air is advancing to replace cooler air.

+ fact: At a stationary front warm air and cold air meet, with neither advancing.

You're not likely to hear a television meteorologist describe the weather system or storm threatening to bring widespread rain or snow as an extratropical cyclone—but chances are it is one. The term applies to any storm that is not a tropical cyclone (or hurricane). Unlike tropical cyclones, these storms contain both warm and cold air masses with fronts as boundaries between them. The temperature contrast between the large masses of cold and warm air supplies the storm's energy. The larger the contrast, the stronger the storm. Extratropical cyclones range in diameter from 600 to 2,500 miles (1,000 to 4,000 km). The fronts usually run like spokes of a wheel from the storm's central area of low pressure.

Winter Storms

Winter storms commonly contain ice, snow, and blizzards, and yet extratropical cyclones that cross North America in the winter can bring thunderstorms, tornadoes, and flooding downpours.

KEY FACTS

Humid winds blowing uphill bring heavy upslope snowstorms to mountains in the West and East.

+ fact: A nor'easter is a winter storm that moves northward along the East Coast of the U.S. and Canada.

+ fact: Alberta clippers are small winter storms that zip from Canada to the East Coast with sharp temperature drops.

From time to time, a strong extratropical cyclone slams into the West Coast from the Pacific Ocean. This results in flooding rain in lower elevations and heavy snow in the mountains. Crossing the Rockies disrupts the storm's surface winds, but as the upper-level winds move over the Great Plains, they stir up surface winds, reviving the winter storm with cold air from Canada and warm air from the Gulf of Mexico.

Some storms move to the Gulf of Mexico and then northeastward along the Atlantic coast; others travel into the Midwest, bringing blizzard conditions. A winter storm's cold front that stretches into the South can produce severe thunderstorms and sometimes tornadoes. A reliable supply of winter snow, of course, is also the lifeblood of ski resorts.

Blizzards

A snowstorm becomes a blizzard when winds reach a speed of 35 mph (56 kph), accompanying falling or blowing snow that reduces visibility to less than a quarter mile (400 m).

> ### KEY FACTS
>
> With few trees to slow winds and reduce blowing snow, blizzards are most common on the Great Plains.
>
> **+ fact:** A severe blizzard has winds faster than 45 mph (72 kph), low visibility, and temperatures of 10°F (-12°C) or lower.
>
> **+ fact:** Snow already on the ground can cause a "ground blizzard" when wind blows it around.

The combination of low temperatures and poor visibility in blowing snow makes blizzard conditions the most dangerous winter weather. The blowing snow creates a "whiteout" when the horizon disappears, no shadows appear, and objects are hidden. Disoriented victims can become lost in places they know well, even between their house and barn. A more common hazard in today's automobile world is a chain-reaction collision often caused by a driver who stops suddenly when visibility drops to zero. In both cases, low temperatures can be fatal for victims who cannot reach warm shelter soon enough. Many blizzard victims die of carbon monoxide poisoning when they run a snowbound car to keep warm and exhaust gas leaks in, or when they use an unvented heat source such as a charcoal grill indoors.

Lake-Effect Snow

Bitter cold air flowing over much warmer water brings heavy snow to areas downwind of the Great Lakes and a few other bodies of water. The lakes are needed for this weather system.

KEY FACTS

Thundersnow occurs more often with lake-effect snow than with other types of snow.

+ fact: Great Lakes snow bands help to bring as much as 200 in (5 m) of snow a year to West Virginia's mountains.

+ fact: Approximately 500 in (13 m) of lake-effect snow from Utah's Great Salt Lake falls on nearby mountains in a year.

Frigid air blowing across lakes that are at least 20°F (11°C) warmer than the air creates cumulus clouds as the warmer lake water evaporates into the cold air. These clouds dump heavy snow as they move inland and over hills. Places downwind of the Great Lakes, such as Buffalo, New York, often have 100 or more inches (2.5 m) of snow a year—double the amount that falls on places at the same latitude not downwind of the lakes. The greatest amounts of lake-effect snow fall early in the season, before the water in the lakes cools. A lake stops making snow if it freezes over.

River Floods

Rivers flood after prolonged heavy rain over a large area or when
deep snow covering a large area melts. Hydrologists can predict
river floods in time for those threatened to flee.

KEY FACTS

A floodplain is flat or
nearly flat land adja-
cent to a river that
floodwaters naturally
cover.

+ fact: Sediments
deposited by previous
floods make flood-
plains prime farmland
with rich soils.

+ fact: A river flood
watch means water is
close to rising above
flood stage; a river
flood warning means
flooding may begin
soon.

River floods are usually slow-motion disasters, with the
highest part of the flood—the crest—moving downstream at less than 10 mph (16 kph). Hydrologists describe
actual and forecast flood heights in relation to the "flood
stage" at particular gauging stations. Flood stage is the
water height at which flooding begins to cause damage
at a location. Because flood stage is different at each station, you cannot rely on figures from upstream to indicate
what your area should expect. Levees—long, earthen banks
that hold back floodwater—sometimes break, which can
quickly enlarge the area covered by floodwater. Because
forecasting isn't perfect, if flooding is predicted for an area
near your home you should be prepared for the flood to be
higher than predicted.

||||||||||||||||||||||||||||||||||||||||||||||||||||||||||||||||||||||||||||||||||||||

Flash Floods

Flash floods, which inundate low-lying areas in less than six hours, are a leading cause of weather deaths in the United States. Intense rainfall or dam failures cause most flash floods.

KEY FACTS

Slowly moving water 2 ft (0.61 m) deep can carry away an SUV-size vehicle.

+ fact: More than half of flash-flood victims were in vehicles driven into water covering a road.

+ fact: A dam failure caused the worst flash flood in U.S. history, killing 2,209 people in Johnstown, Pennsylvania, on May 31, 1889.

Intense rain from thunderstorms or a dying hurricane can create floods that quickly turn usually quiet streams into death traps. In the spring, chunks break off from the ice that has covered a stream. They wash down and pile up into ice dams that can suddenly collapse, creating flash floods. Some of the worst flash floods occur in deserts, where water doesn't soak into the ground. Rain from a thunderstorm too far away to see or hear can race down dry streambeds and catch hikers unaware. Hurricanes and tropical storms that have moved far inland often cause flash floods as well. Those living near streams in hilly or mountainous areas need to be especially aware of the flash-flood danger. A weather radio that turns on and sounds an alarm when a warning is issued can save your life.

Dust Storms

Dust storms, which affect arid regions, fill the air with wind-driven, microscopic dust particles over an extensive area and reduce horizontal visibility to less than $5/8$ of a mile (1 km).

KEY FACTS

The leading edge of a dust storm often looks like a knobby vertical or convex wall.

+ fact: The Arabic word "haboob" is often used for dust storms in the southwestern U.S.

+ fact: Sandstorms do not grow as tall as dust storms because sand particles are larger and heavier. Winds rarely lift sand particles above 50 ft (15 m).

Thunderstorm gust fronts pushing over dry, dusty ground can stir up dust storms. Unlike cold fronts moving into humid areas, which trigger thunderstorms, a cold front in an arid region often lifts dust high into the air. Dust storms can reach a height of roughly 3,000 feet (1,000 m). Cold fronts advancing into dry air create the largest dust storms. In the U.S. Southwest, the dust storm season is May through September. The most severe storms occur when the soil is driest, between April and June, depending on the year's weather. Winds in dust storms are rarely faster than 30 mph (48 kph), but they have been clocked as fast as 62 mph (100 kph). During the 1930s Dust Bowl drought, storms carried dust from the plains to the East Coast.

||||||||||||||||||||||||||||||||||||||||||||||||||||||||||||||||||||||||||||

Volcanic Ash

Volcanic eruptions are not weather events, but can substantially affect the atmosphere. Volcanic ash shot high into the air can stop airplane engines. Some eruptions affect global weather.

KEY FACTS

Between 1982 and 1989, volcanic ash briefly stopped all engines of three Boeing 747s. All three landed safely.

+ fact: Sulfur from the 1991 Mount Pinatubo eruption in the Philippines cooled the Earth for a year.

+ fact: Eruptions in 2010 and 2011 forced *Air Force One* pilots to change President Obama's schedule on three overseas trips.

Both the ash and the gases shot into the air during a volcanic eruption have deleterious effects on weather and daily life. The ash, composed of tiny particles, can block the sun and cool the Earth temporarily. Sulfurous gas shot into the stratosphere during large eruptions forms a haze of sulfuric acid that can block the sunlight and combine with water to form acid rain.

When a jet aircraft runs into a cloud of volcanic ash, the tiny particles invade the spaces between moving parts in the engine and drivetrain and can melt and fuse inside the works. This is why volcanic eruptions such as that of Eyjafjallajökull in Iceland in 2010 call for an emergency interruption of air travel until the atmosphere has cleared, which often takes days.

Air Pressure

Even though we hardly notice the air around us, its pressure is one of the most important forces driving the weather. Unequal air pressures in large masses of air cause the winds to blow.

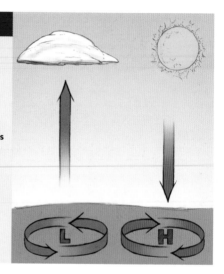

KEY FACTS

At sea level, the air's average pressure is 14.7 lb per in^2.

+ fact: At 18,000 ft (6,000 m) above sea level, air pressure averages 7.25 lb per in^2; half of Earth's air is below that altitude.

+ fact: At 102,000 ft (31,090 m) above sea level, pressure averages 0.147 lb per in^2; 99 percent of Earth's air is below.

Dry air consists of roughly 78 percent nitrogen molecules and 20 percent oxygen, with other gases making up the rest. Air is easily compressed, and the pressure at any altitude depends on the weight of all of the air above pressing down. (That is why air pressure decreases rapidly with increasing altitude.)

The air's molecules are zipping around at roughly 1,000 mph (1,600 kph). As the temperature gets warmer, the movement and speed of the air molecules increases. Fast-moving molecules create pressure pushing in all directions, including up, to oppose the weight of molecules above. We experience the movement of the air as wind. Differences in air pressure at different locations and different altitudes cause winds to blow.

Measuring Air Pressure

Meteorologists measure atmospheric air pressure both at Earth's surface and aloft, because pressure differences between locations determine wind speeds, directions, and weather.

KEY FACTS

The height of mercury in a barometer tube—in inches or millimeters—was the original air pressure measurement.

+ fact: Today the U.S. National Weather Service uses millibars to describe upper air pressures and in surface reports for meteorologists.

+ fact: Canada, like most other nations, uses hectopascals for barometric measurements.

In the late 19th century, as meteorology was becoming a mathematical science, meteorologists began using what are now called hectopascals, a metric unit of pressure, like pounds per square inch, that can easily be used in mathematical formulas. In common parlance, one more likely hears about "inches of mercury," a unit the U.S. National Weather Service uses for surface atmospheric pressure in reports for the public. The phrase harkens back to the mercury barometer, invented by the Italian Evangelista Torricelli in the 1640s. Most weather observers today use electronic devices that sense air pressure, rather than mercury barometers. These devices are at the heart of automated barometers, and hikers can easily carry them.

Why Winds Blow

Winds blow as air moves from areas of high atmospheric pressure toward areas of lower pressure. Because the Earth rotates underneath, the wind follows slightly curved paths.

KEY FACTS

The Coriolis force, named for Gaspard G. Coriolis, describes how Earth's rotation causes winds to follow curved paths.

+ fact: It causes counterclockwise winds around large Northern Hemisphere storms and clockwise winds in the Southern Hemisphere.

+ fact: It has no effect on water draining from a sink or down a toilet.

To see why winds blow, let the air out of a balloon or a bicycle tire and feel the escaping air create a mini-wind as it moves from the high-pressure air inside to the lower-pressure outside air. The same phenomenon happens in the atmosphere on a much larger scale as wind blows from an area of high pressure toward an area of lower pressure. Two factors determine the wind's speed: the difference in pressure and the distance between the two areas. Masses of air close together with distinctly different pressure induce strong winds; masses of air far apart with similar pressure induce little to no wind. Because friction with the ground slows winds near the ground, they are normally slower than winds aloft and also low winds above an ocean or large lake.

Measuring Winds

To describe and predict the weather, meteorologists use various anemometers to measure both wind speed and direction. A wind's direction is named for the direction from which it is blowing.

KEY FACTS

Official surface winds are measured by instruments mounted 33 ft (10 m) above the ground.

+ fact: Wind speeds are calculated as 2-minute averages.

+ fact: A squall is a wind 18 mph (30 kph) faster than the sustained (or steady, underlying) wind. A squall happens suddenly and lasts at least 2 minutes.

The observation of wind speed and direction is an ancient art and a modern science. For many years, most weather stations used cup-and-vane anemometers with spinning cups to measure wind speed and a movable vane to show the wind direction. Snow and ice could disable these, so measurements during severe weather were disrupted. Today, sonic anemometers are becoming standard. They send ultrasound waves between three arms 4 to 8 inches (10 to 20 cm) apart. Winds slow or speed the sound waves, and a processor inside the instrument determines the time it takes for the sound to travel between the arms and uses those findings to calculate wind speed and direction. Sonic anemometers work well in turbulence.

III

Local Winds

Differences in air temperatures over relatively short distances, such as a couple of hundred miles, cause local winds—from gentle sea breezes to the roaring winds that whip up California wildfires.

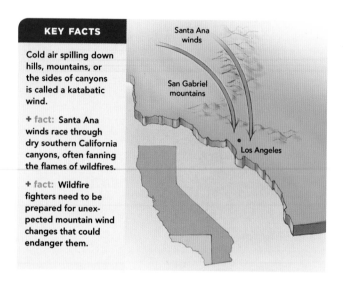

KEY FACTS

Cold air spilling down hills, mountains, or the sides of canyons is called a katabatic wind.

+ fact: Santa Ana winds race through dry southern California canyons, often fanning the flames of wildfires.

+ fact: Wildfire fighters need to be prepared for unexpected mountain wind changes that could endanger them.

Santa Ana winds

San Gabriel mountains

Los Angeles

Local winds occur apart from large air masses and weather systems, caused by the interaction of winds and geography. California's Santa Ana winds begin when dense, cold air builds up east of the Sierras and the southern coastal range. The cold air spills through the canyons, warming as it falls downhill—a local phenomenon that occurs in many places. Sea breezes begin when land warms faster than water. Air rises over the warmed land and air from over the water flows in to replace it. As mountaintops warm during the day, air begins rising, and air from valleys flows uphill to replace it. At night, as the mountaintop air cools, the air becomes heavier and flows down into valleys, making them colder than nearby elevations.

Regional Winds

Various kinds of winds other than parts of tropical or extratropical cyclones can have major regional effects on the weather. These include monsoon winds and chinook winds.

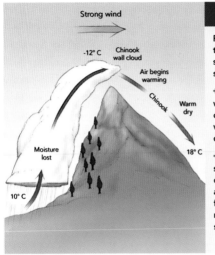

Strong wind

-12° C

Chinook wall cloud

Air begins warming

Chinook

Warm dry

Moisture lost

18° C

10° C

KEY FACTS

Regional wind patterns can vary by season or stay relatively steady year after year.

+ fact: Monsoon winds influence the climate of large areas with strong wet and dry seasons.

+ fact: Low-level jet streams sometimes only 300 ft (90 m) above the ground feed humid air into nighttime thunderstorms on the Plains.

At the intersection of weather systems, landforms, and major bodies of water, regional weather patterns can be expected. Monsoon climates in Asia and in the southwestern United States and adjacent Mexico vary between very dry and very wet seasons. In these regions during the summer, warmed inland air rises and humid winds from the ocean bring humidity, feeding rainstorms. In winter, dry winds blow from inland to the oceans. On the east side of the Rockies, chinook winds warm up as they blow down and melt winter snow. In one case, chinook winds caused temperatures to rise from -54° to 48°F (-48° to 9°C) in 24 hours. Strictly speaking, "monsoon" refers to winds with pronounced seasonal shifts or climates with such shifts. It's also commonly used for heavy summer rain, or even for any heavy rain.

Global Winds

Global-scale winds blow constantly above the Earth, moving warm air out of the tropics and cold air out of the polar regions, setting the stage for smaller weather events that directly affect us.

KEY FACTS

Global wind patterns control movements of air masses around the world.

+ fact: Tropical trade winds blow from the northeast in the Northern Hemisphere, from the southeast in the Southern Hemisphere.

+ fact: Polar easterlies blow from the northeast in the Arctic and from the southeast in the Antarctic.

In the tropics or the polar regions, the winds blow from the east most of the time. In the middle latitudes, north and south, while the general flow is from the west, storms complicate the surface picture with changing wind directions. The winds high aloft, including jet streams—concentrated horizontal, high-altitude winds—move from west to east with deviations to the north and south. Extratropical cyclones travel generally west to east with diversions like those of the jet streams. When tropical cyclones such as hurricanes move into the middle latitudes, their paths begin curving toward a west-to-east direction. Weather forecasters focus a great deal of their attention on measuring and forecasting global-scale winds because they determine the paths and strengths of storms and their winds and precipitation.

Jet Streams

Jet stream paths follow the locations of cold and warm air at the surface and are intimately linked with the movements of cold air toward the Equator and warm air toward the poles.

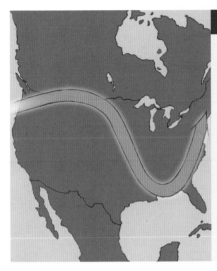

KEY FACTS

Jet stream tailwinds blowing from the west make west-to-east flights quicker than east-to-west flights.

+ fact: Jet streaks are winds sometimes faster than 190 mph (300 kph) embedded in a jet stream.

+ fact: When the jet stream is running generally west to east, the weather should remain calm for a day or two.

Meteorologists define a jet stream as "a relatively narrow river of very strong horizontal winds embedded in the winds that circle Earth aloft." Jet streams skirt the boundaries between deep layers of warm and cold air—fronts on Earth's surface, and often locations of potentially dangerous weather. A wavy jet stream shows that warm air is moving north and cold air south, possibly destined to mix it up in a new storm. Nevertheless, jet streams and other upper air winds steer storms and determine where areas of high and low pressure form at the surface. Jet streams and surface weather dance with one another, neither one always taking the lead. Fair jet stream winds that dip far over the South are a characteristic of strong winter storms.

The Polar Jet Stream

The northern polar jet stream is an upper-atmosphere band of high-speed winds circling above the shifting boundary between cold, dry polar air and warmer, moist mid-latitude air.

KEY FACTS

The polar jet is fastest and farthest south during the coldest parts of winter, farther north in summer.

+ fact: The polar jet stream helps extratropical cyclones form and grow and helps steer them.

+ fact: The Southern Hemisphere's polar jet stream usually circles over the continent of Antarctica all year long.

The polar front separates cold polar air and warm mid-latitude air, but often, polar and mid-latitude air blend with no sharp temperature differences. At such places, the polar jet fades and then forms again where the boundary has larger temperature contrasts. When polar air plunges south, the polar jet turns south and loops around to the north, staying above the warm–cold boundary as a trough. Fast jet streams characterize fierce storms. During the March 12–14, 1963, "superstorm" that paralyzed the East, the polar jet trough dipped all the way over the Gulf of Mexico, and jet stream winds were as fast as 224 mph (360 kph). The extratropical storm below this jet stream had surface winds faster than 74 mph (119 kph).

Atmospheric Rivers

Atmospheric rivers are narrow bands of strong low-level winds—
5,000–8,000 feet (1,500–2,250 m) above oceans—that feed
tropical water vapor to mid-latitude storms.

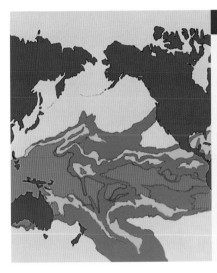

KEY FACTS

Atmospheric rivers supply between a third and a half of all U.S. West Coast precipitation.

+ fact: An atmospheric river from the Pacific Ocean crossed Central America to feed the February 2010 East Coast "Snowmageddon" blizzard.

+ fact: West Coast meteorologists often call atmospheric rivers the "Pineapple Express."

As far back as the 1930s, scientists hypothesized the existence of narrow bands of strong low-level winds that supplied moisture for middle-latitude storms. It took computers and weather satellites to confirm it. In the 1990s, researchers suggested that three to five narrow rivers of air supply 90 percent of the tropical water vapor that reaches the middle latitudes. In 2004, using data collected during airplane flights into these atmospheric rivers and other sources, NOAA scientists confirmed the hypothesis. West Coast forecasters now use these research results to improve forecasts for rain and snow brought by the atmospheric rivers, some of which flow eastward from near Hawaii. Atmospheric rivers also affect Europe and Africa.

Deep Ocean Currents

Water from the Gulf Stream and other currents on the ocean surface are parts of a global conveyor belt that includes underwater currents and transports carbon dioxide and nutrients.

KEY FACTS

Oceanographers estimate that water takes 1,000 years to travel the complete circuit of global currents on and below the surface.

+ fact: Deep ocean water lies more than 6,000 ft (1,800 m) below the surface, where little light penetrates.

+ fact: Deep ocean water is very cold, usually from 32°F to 37°F (0°C to 3°C).

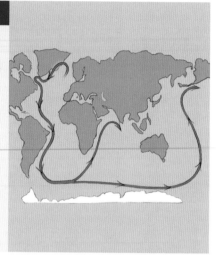

The Gulf Stream is a great river in the ocean that travels northward up the east coast of Mexico, eastward between Florida and Cuba, and northward along the U.S. and Canadian east coast. Water carried north cools and grows denser, with evaporation, leaving behind salt. East of Greenland, this water sinks to form Atlantic deep water, part of the global system of underwater currents. As these currents traverse the deep oceans, they carry organic matter including animal waste and parts of dead plants and animals. The currents also carry carbon dioxide that was absorbed by the water when it was cold. Eventually the water with its nutrients and carbon dioxide upwells along the west coasts of North and South America and Africa, and along parts of the Equator, creating rich areas for sea life.

Surface Ocean Currents

Global winds, such as tropical trade winds, drive oceanic surface currents. The currents carry heat from the tropics to the middle and polar latitudes, with important effects on climate.

KEY FACTS

The warmth of the Gulf Stream (pictured) adds energy to storms crossing it, increasing their wind speeds.

+ fact: Off the U.S. Atlantic coastline, the Gulf Stream moves as fast as 5.6 mph (9 kph).

+ fact: The California current, which moves south along the U.S. West Coast, helps keep coastal waters cool.

Earth's ocean currents form oceanwide gyres—clockwise in the Northern Hemisphere, counterclockwise in the Southern. Through the 20th century, scientists had thought that these currents did most of the work of transporting heat toward the poles. Now, however, there is strong evidence that forces in the atmosphere in the Northern Hemisphere are responsible for carrying 78 percent of the heat moved toward the north. Ocean currents do most of the work in the Southern Hemisphere, carrying 92 percent of the heat moving toward Antarctica. Researchers are also finding strong evidence that the Gulf Stream doesn't do as much to keep Europe warm as previously thought. Southwest winds also play an important role in warming Europe during the winter.

El Niño

El Niño, which happens every few years, occurs when unusually warm tropical surface water flows into parts of the Pacific Ocean. The shifting of warm water has global effects.

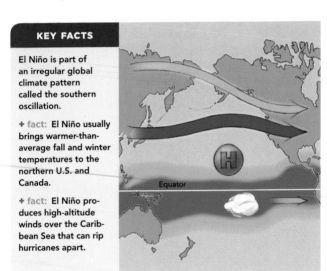

KEY FACTS

El Niño is part of an irregular global climate pattern called the southern oscillation.

+ fact: El Niño usually brings warmer-than-average fall and winter temperatures to the northern U.S. and Canada.

+ fact: El Niño produces high-altitude winds over the Caribbean Sea that can rip hurricanes apart.

Equator

Air flowing out of the tops of Pacific thunderstorms feeds global winds. El Niño pushes these thunderstorms farther east and disrupts jet streams downstream across the Americas. These disruptions, in turn, shift normal patterns of rain, dryness, and storminess as far away as Africa. In North America, the effect is increased rain in normally drier areas and noticeably arid weather in areas that usually get rain. An El Niño occurred in 1957–58, the International Geophysical Year, and scientists began to understand the connection between events that were long assumed to be unconnected. Today, measurements taken in the Pacific Ocean help to predict coming El Niño events, which can have serious economic repercussions.

La Niña

La Niña, the counterpart to El Niño, is characterized by unusually cold sea-surface temperatures in the eastern, tropical Pacific as the ocean's warmest water moves to the west.

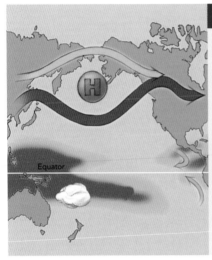

Equator

KEY FACTS

Paths of the subtropical and polar jet streams are more variable during La Niña years.

+ fact: La Niña years tend to have warmer-than-normal winters in the southeastern U.S. and cooler-than-normal winters in the northwestern U.S. and Canada.

+ fact: La Niña increases the odds of a hurricane hitting the U.S. Atlantic or Gulf coast.

Also part of the southern oscillation, La Niña is a Pacific Ocean phenomenon with global implications. El Niño begins with the shift of warm waters in the tropical Pacific to the east, and La Niña begins with enhanced upwelling of deep ocean waters along the South American coast, thus cooling this part of the ocean. Stronger trade winds push the warmest water to the west along with the thunderstorms above it. As with El Niño, winds flowing out of the tops of these storms affect jet streams, but in different patterns. In the southeastern region of the United States, where El Niño would bring downpours, La Niña generally brings drought. Both El Niño and La Niña tend to peak during winter in the Northern Hemisphere. In 2011 some scientists linked that year's tornado outbreaks to La Niña, but other scientists disputed this. The question is far from settled.

Arctic Oscillation

The Arctic Oscillation (AO) is an irregular swing between opposite air pressure and wind patterns centered on the Arctic. It strongly affects winter weather in eastern North America.

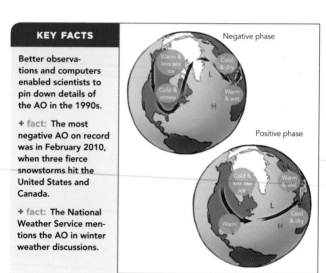

KEY FACTS

Better observations and computers enabled scientists to pin down details of the AO in the 1990s.

+ fact: The most negative AO on record was in February 2010, when three fierce snowstorms hit the United States and Canada.

+ fact: The National Weather Service mentions the AO in winter weather discussions.

The Arctic Oscillation's positive phase features lower air pressures over the Arctic and strong upper air winds around latitude 55° N, which blocks cold outbreaks from hitting the northeastern United States and Canada. The AO's negative phase includes higher air pressure over the Arctic and weaker upper air winds around 55° N, which allows more cold outbreaks to hit the Northeast. The AO can switch between phases in days, but sometimes one phase dominates for long periods. From the early 1960s until the mid-1990s, the AO was positive more often than negative. Since then, the AO has switched phases more often, with extreme negative phases dominating the winters of 2009–10 and 2010–11, which were cold and snowy in the Northeast.

Atlantic Multidecadal Oscillation

The Atlantic Multidecadal Oscillation (AMO) refers to swings in the surface temperature of the Atlantic Ocean between the Equator and Greenland that influence weather widely.

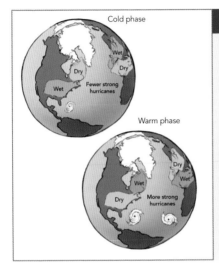

Cold phase

Warm phase

KEY FACTS

During a cold AMO phase, North America and the Caribbean experience fewer hurricanes.

+ fact: A cold phase from 1971 to 1994 averaged only 1.125 major hurricanes a year; a warm phase from 1995 to 2012 averaged 4 major hurricanes a year.

+ fact: The Dust Bowl drought of the 1930s occurred during a warm phase.

The Atlantic Ocean seems to swing between warm and cool phases lasting 20 to 40 years. Its average temperature during a warm phase is approximately 1°F (0.55°C) above that of a cool phase. Spread out over the ocean, this is a lot of heat, and it can energize hurricanes and affect patterns of high and low atmospheric pressure. Even pressure patterns far from the ocean appear linked to this cycle: African droughts in cold phases, North American droughts in warm phases. Paleoclimatic proxies, such as tree rings and ice cores, show that the AMO has been occurring for at least 1,000 years. It is not an effect of current climate change. Subtle changes in the speed of the Gulf Stream drive the AMO. When the Gulf Stream slows, the Atlantic Ocean cools slightly; when it speeds up, the Atlantic warms up.

Stationary Fronts

Like all fronts, stationary fronts separate large air masses with different densities—usually caused by temperature differences. Neither air mass is advancing along a stationary front.

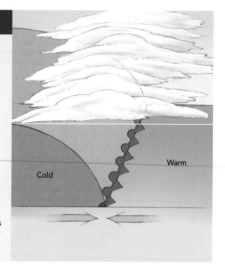

KEY FACTS

Map symbol: Red and blue lines with alternating red semicircles facing colder air and blue triangles facing warmer air

+ fact: Any kind of front can become stationary if upper air winds begin blowing parallel to the front.

+ fact: In the spring and fall, stationary fronts can lie across the Southeast for days at a time.

Cold

Warm

A stationary front forms when either a cold or a warm front stops moving. Warm, humid air can ride over the front to supply humidity for clouds and precipitation on the cold side of the front. Upper air disturbances can travel along the front, creating clouds and precipitation for days at a time. If an upper air pattern that encourages air to rise moves overhead, a low-pressure area will form on the front.

Its counterclockwise winds around the low—in the Northern Hemisphere—begin pushing the warm air toward the north or northwest and the cold air toward the south or southeast to begin organizing an extratropical cyclone.

||||||||||||||||||||||||||||||||||||||||||||||||||||||||||||||||||||||||||||||||||||

Cold Fronts

A cold front is the leading edge at the surface of a mass of cold air that is replacing warmer air. Showers and thunderstorms and wind shifts accompany most cold fronts.

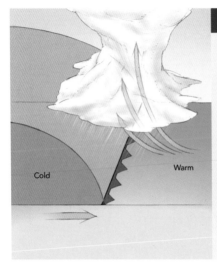

Cold

Warm

KEY FACTS

Map symbol: A blue line with blue triangles pointing in the direction of movement

+ fact: A "backdoor" cold front moves into the northeastern U.S. from the northeast instead of the northwest like most cold fronts.

+ fact: Frontogenesis is a front's formation; frontolysis is a front's dissipation or weakening.

As a cold front advances, the colder and denser air behind it wedges under the less dense warmer air, lifting it. If the warm air is moist and the atmosphere is unstable—the usual case in North America—this lifting forms showers and thunderstorms. These thunderstorms can be very strong, even severe, especially in the spring when the atmosphere is often unstable.

During the winter, when a cold front reinforces dry, cold air already in place, little snow or rain might fall. A reliable sign that a cold front has passed is a wind shift from southwesterly to northwesterly. The coldest air is often a few miles behind the front.

Warm Fronts

A warm front is the boundary where warm air is replacing colder air. The clouds associated with a warm front can be more than 700 miles (1,100 km) ahead of the front.

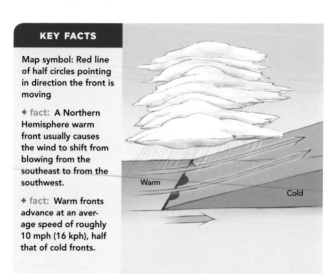

KEY FACTS

Map symbol: Red line of half circles pointing in direction the front is moving

+ fact: A Northern Hemisphere warm front usually causes the wind to shift from blowing from the southeast to from the southwest.

+ fact: Warm fronts advance at an average speed of roughly 10 mph (16 kph), half that of cold fronts.

Warm

Cold

An advancing warm front doesn't arrive with the drama of a strong cold front, but it affects a much larger area. Because warm air is lighter than cold air, a warm front's air rises over the cold air. The warm air can be 6,000 feet (1,800 m) above the ground and 150–200 miles (249–320 km) ahead of the front. As a warm front approaches, you will first see high cirrus clouds, which become cirrostratus or cirrocumulus. These thicken and descend to become altocumulus and altostratus clouds. Snow or rain could then begin, as when you see nimbostratus clouds. After the surface front passes, the sky will begin clearing and temperatures will warm up.

Occluded Fronts

Unlike stationary, cold, and warm fronts that divide two air masses with contrasting densities, occluded fronts are more complex. They separate three air masses: cold, cool, and warm.

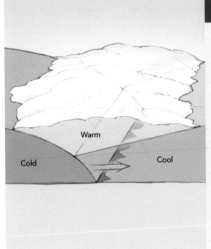

Warm

Cold

Cool

KEY FACTS

Map symbol: Alternating purple cold-front triangles and warm-front half circles

+ fact: Occluded fronts are the most common kind of fronts moving into western North America from the Pacific Ocean.

+ fact: More detailed observations and computer models are helping meteorologists better understand occlusions.

In a "cold" occlusion, the surface boundary separates very cold and cold air with the warm air appearing to have been shoved up by the very cold air to intersect the very cold air aloft. In a "warm" occlusion, cool air is riding over very cold air with the warm air above the cold air. Many textbooks say "warm air catching up with cold air" forms occlusions. Some meteorologists today, using more complete observations and computer models, say a better description involves the warm front and cold front wrapping around a storm's low-pressure center after the warm front separates from the low-pressure center.

Dry Line

A dry line, like a front, separates air masses of different densities. These differences are in humidity, not temperature, as with most fronts. Dry lines occur on the Southwestern Plains.

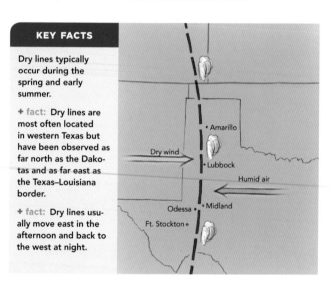

KEY FACTS

Dry lines typically occur during the spring and early summer.

+ fact: Dry lines are most often located in western Texas but have been observed as far north as the Dakotas and as far east as the Texas–Louisiana border.

+ fact: Dry lines usually move east in the afternoon and back to the west at night.

The air masses that are in conflict along a dry line are very dry, warm, or hot air moving east from the Southwest and humid hot air moving west from the Gulf of Mexico. Because humid air is less dense than dry air of the same temperature, the dry air pushes under the humid air much as cold air shoves under warm air. This can trigger showers and thunderstorms, sometimes severe thunderstorms with tornadoes, much as advancing cold fronts cause storms. Dry air is denser than humid air because added water molecules are lighter than the nitrogen and oxygen molecules they replace as humidity increases. Thunderstorms tend to form where the dry line bulges and pushes air up. These storms usually are more isolated and severe than those that form elsewhere because they aren't competing with other storms.

Upper Air Troughs

Upper air troughs are elongated areas of low atmospheric pressures relative to adjacent air pressures at particular altitudes. They influence the locations, strengths, and paths of storms.

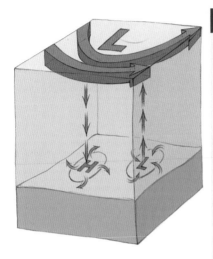

KEY FACTS

Air rises on the eastern side of a Northern Hemisphere trough aloft, which helps surface storms to intensify.

+ fact: Air sinks on the west side of a Northern Hemisphere trough, creating a dry, high-pressure area below.

+ fact: A trough aloft forms when the air below is colder than air on either side of the trough.

Weather forecasters pay particular attention to troughs aloft because they have a major influence on the weather below by helping storms to form or intensify. When you hear broadcast meteorologists talk about possible bad effects on local weather from "upper air energy" or an "upper air disturbance," they are probably talking about a trough or a "cutoff low." The low formed when the southern end of a trough was pinched off to become an upper air low-pressure area that is disconnected from the upper air wind flow. Cutoffs can hang around for days in the same place or even move to the west, causing cloudy skies and precipitation before they dissipate. A trough and an upper air ridge—where winds aloft turn to the north and back to the south—make one of the three to seven meandering waves that circle Earth.

The Aleutian Low

The Aleutian low is a semipermanent area of low atmospheric pressure that strengthens each fall and fades during spring. From fall through spring, it steers storms into the Pacific Northwest.

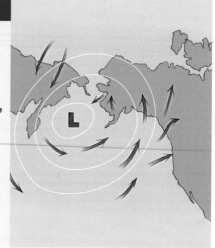

KEY FACTS

In winter, the Aleutian low regularly sends storms into the Pacific Northwest with only brief breaks.

+ fact: During an El Niño in the tropics, the Aleutian low tends to be deeper and spins off stronger storms.

+ fact: A weak Aleutian low can occur any year, but it is especially likely during a strong La Niña.

The Aleutian low forms each winter as Alaska begins turning frigid, leaving the Pacific Ocean around the Aleutian Islands the warmest surface in the region. Because the water is relatively warm, air over it begins rising, forming a low pressure center that continues until spring when the land warms up. Storms that form or strengthen here often have winds faster than 50 mph (80 kph), which create huge waves that surfers in Hawaii love—some as tall as 65 feet (20 m) high when they head south. Waves heading north are the ones that make the Discovery Channel's *Deadliest Catch* show exciting. The Aleutian low's Atlantic Ocean counterpart is the Icelandic low. In summer when the Aleutian low is weak, the North Pacific high moves north so it is west of California, strengthens, and keeps the West Coast mostly dry.

The Bermuda High

While the Bermuda high is centered far out over the Atlantic Ocean, it has several effects on North American weather, including steering Atlantic hurricanes toward or away from the U.S.

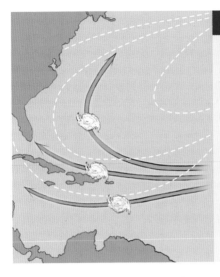

KEY FACTS

The high doesn't always protect Bermuda from hurricanes. One hurricane, on average, hits Bermuda every seven years or so.

+ fact: In 2004 the high was farther west than usual and steered a record four hurricanes to Florida.

+ fact: In winter and spring, the high is centered over the Azores as the Azores high.

Bermuda is in the global belt of high atmospheric pressure and mostly calm winds around latitude 30° N, where air rising in tropical thunderstorms descends to maintain high atmospheric pressure. Winds flowing clockwise out of the high contribute to the easterly tropical trade winds and often feed warm humid air into the eastern United States in the summer, especially the Southeast. The clockwise winds around the high steer hurricanes. Slight changes in the strength and position of the high help to determine whether a hurricane heads northward between Bermuda and the United States, hits the Northeast, the Southeast, or heads into the Gulf of Mexico. Predicting how the Bermuda high and winds around it will change is a major aspect of forecasting the likely paths of hurricanes in the Atlantic Ocean.

Ground/Radiation Fog

Radiation fog forms when heat radiates from the Earth overnight, cooling the air enough for its water vapor to begin condensing into tiny water drops. The fog forms next to the ground.

KEY FACTS

Ground fog is usually thickest before sunrise, when evaporation starts.

+ fact: Fog cuts visibility to 0.6 mi (1 km); mist cuts visibility to less than 6 mi (9 km).

+ fact: The NWS reports "fog" when it is less than 20 ft (6 m) deep, and "shallow fog" when it is less than 6 ft (2 m) deep.

Radiation fog, also called ground fog, is most likely to form when the sky has been mostly clear all night, which allows the most heat to radiate away from Earth. Winds should also be calm or nearly calm because stronger winds will mix the coldest air next to the ground with slightly warmer air a few feet higher. Chances of fog are much better when rain has soaked the ground the day before. Water from soaked ground evaporates into the air. The added moisture allows water vapor to began condensing at a higher temperature than it would in drier air. The fog usually begins evaporating shortly after sunrise. Afternoon rain that leaves water on the ground to evaporate, a sky that clears overnight, and 5 to 10 mph (8 to 16 kph) winds combine to make morning fog likely.

Steam Fog

The wisps of "steam" you see rising from ponds or lakes in the fall when the year's first cold air arrives are "steam" fog, which needs a combination of warm water and cold air to form.

KEY FACTS

Steam fog forms when warm water evaporates into cold air, making the air humid enough to form fog.

+ fact: All year, steam fog forms above thermal ponds in Yellowstone National Park.

+ fact: Steam fog begins a few inches above the water because the rising air needs to cool enough to form fog.

Arctic air that begins moving south over North America in the fall is too dry to form fog without some help. This help comes when it flows over ponds, lakes, or rivers, and some of the relatively warm water evaporates into the cold air, giving it enough humidity for condensation to begin at the air's current temperature. Steam fog that forms over an ocean is called "sea smoke." When frigid air moves over much warmer water, the rising fog can create steam devils up to 1,600 feet (500 m) high. In a case studied, the water was 39°F (22°C) warmer than the air. Most fog forms in light winds, but steam devils illustrate the turbulence associated with steam fog. It forms under extreme temperature differences between warm water and frigid air. The Great Lakes are a prime location for steam devils.

Advection Fog

Advection fog forms when winds push humid air over ground or water cold enough to chill the air to a temperature that causes its humidity to condense into tiny fog drops.

KEY FACTS

Coastal advection fog supplies 30 to 40 percent of moisture to California's redwoods.

+ fact: Warm Gulf Stream air advected over the nearby Labrador Current makes Newfoundland's Grand Banks one of Earth's foggiest places.

+ fact: Summer breezes across the cool Great Lakes form persistent advection fog.

Meteorologists use the word "advection" for the horizontal transport of meteorological property such as temperature or moisture. Some of North America's most troublesome fog is the widespread, dense, and long-lasting advection fog. It occurs across the Midwest created when warm, humid air moves north from the Gulf of Mexico. As the warm air passes over cool ground or water, the temperature drops to dewpoint and condensation may occur. The term advection refers to the horizontal movement of air.

Southern California's famous "May Gray" and "June Gloom" marine layer is advection fog that is formed when tropical air from the Pacific Ocean flows over the cold California Current near the coast. This type of fog normally rolls in early in the morning and dissipates during the day.

Ice Fog

Ice fog is made of tiny ice crystals that float in the air, just as water drops do in ordinary fog. It forms only at temperatures below -30°F (-35°C).

KEY FACTS

Ice fog particles are small enough for 10 to fit side by side on the edge of a piece of paper.

+ fact: When the air is -40°F (-40°C), water from a car's tailpipe drops from 250°F (121°C) to the air temperature in less than 10 seconds.

+ fact: Ice fog is sometimes called pogonip, from a Shoshone word for "cloud."

Because ice fog needs such low temperatures, it occurs only in the northern provinces of Canada, in inland and northern Alaska, and in some high elevations in the Pacific Northwest. Ice fog can also be called frozen fog, but it should be distinguished from freezing fog, which is made of water drops that instantly freeze when they touch anything. Ice fog forms only in extremely dry air, but in built-up places such as Fairbanks, Alaska, exhaust from vehicles adds water vapor to the air, and that can instantly become tiny ice fog particles. In Fairbanks, the resulting thick ice fog—with other pollutants added— can drop visibility to near zero and push air quality to unhealthy levels. A few miles from the city's traffic, the air can be clear.

Natural Haze

Haze is a collection of very fine, widely dispersed, solid or liquid particles suspended in the air. They turn the sky milky white and subdue colors. Hazes can be natural or occur from human activities.

KEY FACTS

The chemical properties of haze particles can change the effects of the haze on the view.

+ fact: Volatile organic compounds from trees help to form a bluish haze: That's what makes the Blue Ridge Mountains blue.

+ fact: Salt particles in the air affect beach scenes, creating a low, white haze in the daytime and red sunsets.

Haze has a direct effect on how far we can see, because its particles are just the right size in relation to wavelengths of light to scatter or absorb some colors, which reduces visibility. We often think of any such obstruction to visibility as pollution, but it's not always the case. Haze is sometimes air pollution—particles or gases in the air added by human activity with the potential for harming life or property. But haze can be natural, coming from a volcanic eruption, or smoke from wildfires started by lightning, or dust. Water vapor can condense on dry haze particles and make them larger, which further reduces visibility by scattering or absorbing more light. This condition most likely occurs in the morning or evening, when relative humidity is higher.

Pollution Haze or Smog

Photochemical smog, a brownish haze, is a mixture of hundreds of hazardous chemicals. It is most often found over and downwind of cities. It is unpleasant and unsightly, and can be deadly.

KEY FACTS

Henry Antoine des Voeux, a London physician, coined "smog" for smoke and fog in 1905.

+ fact: Reactions involving sunlight, nitrogen oxides, and volatile organic compounds produce photochemical smog.

+ fact: Ozone near the Earth's surface is a pollutant, but ozone in the stratosphere blocks dangerous ultraviolet light.

An inversion—air aloft that's warmer than ground-level air—sets the stage for smog: It blocks warm air from rising, so that it cannot be replaced by clean air descending from above. At times, an inversion can trap polluted air over a city for days as more smog brews. In addition to the visible smog, invisible pollutants are at work, including carbon monoxide and extremely small particles so tiny that they travel deep into the lungs, causing damage that can be fatal. Rain and snow wash pollutants out of the air, but civilization often produces so much pollution that this natural cleaning process cannot keep up. Volatile organic compounds (with noticeable odors) from industrial and natural sources, such as trees, are one (but far from the only) component of smog.

Rainbows

When sunlight, a mix of colors, enters and reflects out of a water drop, it bends, with each color bending at a different angle. The light reflects off the drop's back and is visible as separate colors.

KEY FACTS

In 1637, French philosopher René Descartes discovered how refractions in individual drops form rainbows.

+ fact: Rainbows may be partial if it is raining only in the part of the sky directly opposite the sun.

+ fact: Large raindrops create bright rainbows with sharp colors; small drops make washed-out colors.

Rainbows are visible phenomena, but are not actual objects, and your eyes must be in the right relationship between the sun and raindrops to see them. If the sun isn't directly in back of your head, you aren't looking at a rainbow. (You could be seeing iridescence or a circumzenithal arc.) Light hits the raindrops, which act like tiny prisms, dividing light into its component colors as it shines back out. Double rainbows are made by the same raindrops that make the primary rainbow. You often hear that rainbows have seven colors, but a rainbow has the whole range of colors from red at the top to violet at the bottom of a primary bow. Usually we see fewer than seven colors.

Sun's light rays

40°
42°

Fogbows and Moonbows

A fogbow is created the same way as a rainbow but by water drops in fog, not rain. Rain or a waterfall can disperse the light of a full moon to create a moonbow. Both are rare.

Fogbows are much fainter than rainbows because light is traveling through much smaller water drops, and their colors aren't as sharp as those of rainbows. They usually appear white, sometimes with faint red and blue. Moonbows will occur only when the moon is full and brightest, but not directly overhead: For a moonbow to occur, the moon cannot be more than 42°, or a little less than halfway up from the horizon to the zenith. As with a sunlit rainbow, the moon must be behind your head as you look into the rain or waterfall, where drops of water are bending the incoming light and dividing it like a prism into its component colors. Full moons set around sunrise, and the hours before sunrise are the best time to look for a moonbow.

Sun Dogs

"Sun dog" is an informal name for a parhelion, a splotch of light seen on one or both sides of the sun. They are the most common visual display caused by ice crystals floating in the air.

KEY FACTS

Sun dogs are brightest when the sun is low.

+ fact: Some Arctic people are said to call them "the sun's dogs."

+ fact: In 1461, King Henry VI reportedly inspired his troops to win a battle by calling the sun and two sun dogs they saw the Holy Trinity: God was on their side.

+ fact: Sun dogs appear in many different climates.

Parhelia—the plural of parhelion—are colorful, glowing spots formed by light bending as it enters and leaves plate-shaped, hexagonal ice crystals floating facedown in cirrus clouds. In most parts of the world, sun dogs appear at a 22° angle higher than the sun and on one or both sides of the sun. They can appear as often as a couple of times a week, most visibly when the sun is close to the horizon. Once you start looking for sun dogs when cirrus clouds are in the sky, you might be amazed how often you see them (and you can amaze others by pointing them out, and explaining how ice causes them).

Atmospheric Halos

Arcs or circles shining around the sun or moon, atmospheric halos are the visible effects of light passing through ice crystals in the atmosphere.

KEY FACTS

Scientists call all atmospheric displays caused by ice crystals "halos."

+ fact: A 22° halo is caused by randomly oriented, hexagonal columns—crystals shaped like tiny pencils, scattered through the atmosphere.

+ fact: Some atmospheric halos glow with colors, ranging from red on the inside to blue on the outside.

Ice crystals hanging in cirrus clouds high in the upper troposphere, 3 to 6 miles (5 to 10 km) above the ground, can create visible arcs, circles, and spots by reflecting and refracting light. As in rainbows, the white light is sometimes split into its component colors. Atmospheric halos have been observed and interpreted for millennia, sometimes as signals of weather to come and sometimes as spiritual messages. Today, the optics of the phenomenon are fully understood, but the marvel of halos remains. On January 11, 1999, for example, observers at the South Pole saw 22 different kinds of halos.

Circumzenithal Arc

A circumzenithal arc is a ring directly overhead or almost directly overhead. It is easier to miss than most other halos because you're not likely to look straight up.

KEY FACTS

If you see a sun dog with the sun 15° to 25° above the horizon, look straight up. You might see a circumzenithal arc.

+ fact: When looking at halos and other sun phenomena, you need to shield your eyes from the sun.

+ fact: Regular skywatchers might see a circumzenithal arc 25 times a year.

Unlike most halos that appear white, maybe with a tinge of color, a circumzenithal arc is colorful. It has been described as an "upside-down rainbow." The colors normally range from blue on the inside to red on the outside—the side toward the sun. Bending of light rays as they enter and leave ice crystals causes all halos. Such refraction separates sunlight into its colors.

Hexagonal columns, each shaped like a pencil, cause circumzenithal arcs when light enters the top face and leaves through one of the sides. The arc forms only when the sun is lower than 32.2° above the horizon. The arc can be wider than shown here. Colloquially, some call them fire rainbows because they sometimes have a fiery look, but they are not rainbows.

Moon Dogs

A moon dog is the lunar version of a sun dog: a glowing spot or pair of spots visible alongside the bright full moon, created by moonlight passing through ice crystals in the atmosphere.

KEY FACTS

The scientific name for a moon dog is parase-lene (plural parasele-nae), meaning "beside the moon."

+ fact: You see little color in moon dogs because they aren't bright enough to acti-vate your eye's cones, which perceive color.

+ fact: A few nights before and after the full moon it is bright enough to make halos.

Because the moon is a source of light in the sky, it produces halos, including moon dogs, just as the sun does. If ice crystals are present in the atmosphere, moonlight coming through may reflect and refract that light, making it visible in these attractive patterns. Moon dogs and halos are much dimmer than those generated by the sun, because all of the moon's light is reflected. Moon halos are more common than moon dogs. Folklore says that a ring around the moon means that rain is on the way. Maybe. Cirrus clouds that create halos are sometimes, but not always, a sign that a warm front is arriving with rain.

Coronas

You see a corona when the sun or moon shines through thin clouds. It appears as a bright center (the sun or moon) surrounded by one or more reddish or brownish rings.

KEY FACTS

A safe way to view a corona around the sun is to look at its reflection in water.

+ fact: Coronas are often seen in altocumulus or altostratus clouds, which are often part of a storm that could bring rain or snow.

+ fact: Coronas have colors when the cloud drops or ice crystals in the cloud are the same size.

Rainbows and halos are visible when water or ice causes the refraction, or bending, of light rays. Coronas (and other sky phenomena such as iridescence) are visible when water drops in the atmosphere cause the diffraction, or spreading and rejoining, of light rays. Coronas are created by smaller water particles than halos, and they are more commonly seen. Sometimes the physics of the light and water droplets is such that colors are visible. When that happens, red is always the outermost color and sometimes the only color. This use of the word should not be confused with its astronomical meaning, referring to the sun's outer atmosphere. A corona's size depends on the diameters of the cloud drops. Small drops produce large coronas. A corona is clearest when the drops are mostly the same size.

Crepuscular Rays

Close to sunset or sunrise, beams of light will often appear as if they are radiating from the sun, coming through breaks in the clouds and fanning out as they come down to Earth.

KEY FACTS

"Crepuscular" is derived from the Latin word *crepusculum*, which means "twilight."

+ fact: People sometimes say "the sun is drawing water," harking back to the ancient Greek belief that sunbeams draw water into the sky.

+ fact: Crepuscular rays are often red or yellow because air molecules selectively scatter blue light.

You see the "beams" of light—called crepuscular rays—because haze, dust, or tiny water drops floating in the air scatter the sun's light in all directions, including essentially parallel lines toward you. From your vantage point, the beams appear to converge in the sky because of the principles of perspective—the same reason the edges of a straight road appear to converge at the horizon. While you're looking at crepuscular rays, turn around, put the sun at your back, and if the sky is clear, you may see "anticrepuscular" rays converging on the "antisolar" point opposite the sun. If the air were perfectly clean, you would not see crepuscular rays. Light from the sun is traveling a straight path from the sun to Earth, not toward you. Tiny particles such as dust scatter light in all directions, including toward your eyes.

Sun and Light Pillars

Near sunrise or sunset, bright columns of light appear to shoot above and below the sun: sun pillars. On a frigid night, you may see columns shooting into the sky from streetlights.

KEY FACTS

The second and third brightest objects in the sky, the moon and Venus, also form light pillars.

+ fact: Crystals for light pillars form only at temperatures below freezing.

+ fact: Gusty winds can rearrange a light pillar's crystals, making it shimmer like an aurora overhead.

Halos become visible when the sun's light rays bend as they pass through ice crystals, but both sun pillars and light pillars emerge when light reflects off ice crystals instead. This is why they are the color of the source of the light—red beaming above the red setting sun near the horizon—instead of being mostly white. Sun pillars usually extend at an angle of only 5° to 10° above the sun. Light pillars form on clear nights that are cold enough to form ice-crystal fog, composed of tiny crystals. This form of fog is also called diamond dust.

Auroras

Auroras, shimmering curtains of green and brown-red lights seen high in the skies of Earth's far north and far south, are visible evidence of our planet's direct connections to the sun.

KEY FACTS

Auroras follow the 11-year solar cycle and tend to be more frequent in the late autumn and early spring.

+ fact: Around the Arctic Circle in northern Norway and Alaska, auroras are visible almost every night.

+ fact: Auroras are seen only once or twice a century over the southern United States.

Solar winds send energetic charged particles from the sun toward the Earth, attracted especially into the atmosphere over the Arctic and Antarctic by the electromagnetic fields of our planet. Here they smash into the atoms of nitrogen and oxygen, the primary constituents of our atmosphere. These collisions send off photons, which create visible light: the eerie, shimmering, sky-filled curtains of the aurora borealis (northern lights) over the Arctic and aurora australis (southern lights) over Antarctica. The auroras are the only visible aspect of space weather: the many effects on Earth of high-energy particles from the sun, which can disrupt satellites.

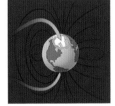

Iridescence

Iridescent clouds have washed-out, mostly pastel colors visible on some or all of the cloud. Most often, iridescence appears as a border of red and green along the edge of a cloud formation.

KEY FACTS

Every cloud does not have a silver lining: Some have colored iridescent linings; most have no lining at all.

+ fact: Iridescence can be seen in cirrus, altocumulus, cirrocumulus, and lenticular clouds.

+ fact: Iridescence is more visible if the sun is shaded, either by a denser cloud or deliberately by the viewer stepping behind a tree or building.

Sometimes a cloud will seem to show colors similar to a rainbow contoured to the shape of the cloud. Iridescence—the appearance of colors within or along the borders of a cloud—is caused by tiny water drops or small ice crystals, each individually scattering and diffracting light. The optics that create an iridescent cloud are similar to those that create colors on the surface of an oily puddle. Iridescence develops primarily in thin clouds positioned relatively close to the sun. The colors can be very subtle or rather bright, but they will shift and change quickly. The colors you see in an iridescent cloud can be considered fragments of a corona. Unlike coronas that form in clouds or parts of clouds with drops of relatively uniform size, iridescence shows that the cloud is made of drops with different sizes.

Glories

From your window seat on an airplane just above the clouds, you're casually looking out when you see the shadow of your airplane with a ring of light around it. You're looking at a glory.

KEY FACTS

Before flying became common, the best way to see a glory was from a mountain above cloud tops.

+ fact: You sometimes see a glory around the shadow of your head on a cloud.

+ fact: The shadow glory is called a "Brocken spectre," for the highest peak in Germany's Harz Mountains, known for its glories.

A glory, a colorful halo encircling a shadow in the clouds below the viewer's eye level, is not as simple as light scattered back from the cloud to create colored rings. A phenomenon that appears at the antisolar point—directly opposite the sun in relation to the viewer—a glory is visible only to a person positioned between the sun and the top layer of clouds.

This optical phenomenon must be explained by a more complex physical process than simple reflection or diffraction. Physicists are still unsure of the process, and determining the atmospheric optics of glories is a challenge to this day. Their findings could apply to climate science because of the possibility that clouds reflect more sunlight than previously thought.

Green Flash

As you watch the sun set over an open-water horizon, you may see a green flash: a momentary change in the color of the sun to green before it disappears.

KEY FACTS

The best place to see a green flash is from a view at a high elevation above an ocean horizon.

+ fact: Looking for a green flash with binoculars or an SLR camera viewfinder can permanently damage your eyes.

+ fact: In Antarctica, where the sun rises and sets slowly—once a year for each—a green flash can last a half hour.

In locations where a large lake, bay, or the ocean stretches out to the west, far as the eye can see, many people gather in early evening to try to catch a glimpse of the elusive green flash. It may look like a green spot for a second or two or like a green ray shooting up from the sun. There is a physical explanation for this. The atmosphere refracts or bends light's different wavelengths in a standard order of colors. As the sun slips below the horizon, the red disappears first, then a second or so later the yellow, green, and finally blue and violet disappear. Because air scatters blue and violet the most, these colors don't reach your eye. But green might reach you, enhanced as a mirage caused by a layer of warm air over a relatively cool ocean.

Twilight

Twilight is the transition between night and day: from the time light first appears in the morning until sunrise, and from the time the sun reaches the horizon until light fades from the sky.

KEY FACTS

The time from first twilight to dark is 72 minutes.

+ fact: The brightest stars and planets are visible during civil twilight if the sky is clear.

+ fact: The sky turns brilliant colors at twilight because the visible light has traveled through more atmosphere, scattering blue and violet rays, leaving red and yellow.

Twilight—the time between last or first light and the brightness of day—has been defined in many ways. Civil twilight is the period when the sun's center is between the horizon and 6° below the horizon, and the ambient light is usually still bright enough for outdoor activities. Nautical twilight is the period when the sun's center is between 6° and 12° below the horizon, and shapes are visible but not distinct. Astronomical twilight is the period when the sun's center is between 12° and 18° below the horizon. After that, twilight ends, and it is dark. The term "twilight" can also be applied to the same periods of time as the sun is rising.

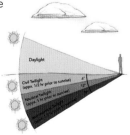

Daylight

Civil Twilight
(appx. 1/2 hr prior to sunrise)   6°

Nautical Twilight
(appx. 1 hr to sunrise)   12°

Thermal Inversions

A thermal inversion (usually just called an inversion) is a layer of warm air above colder air. Temperatures normally decrease with altitude, which makes a thermal inversion unusual.

KEY FACTS

Cold air flowing into valleys pushes up warm air, creating inversions.

+ fact: An inversion caused the 1948 pollution episode in Donora, Pennsylvania, that killed 20 people and sickened hundreds.

+ fact: August inversions at the South Pole can make surface temperatures 70°F (39°C) colder than those 1,000 ft (305 m) above.

Surface inversions form in winter when heat radiates away from Earth faster than solar warmth can replace it. The strongest inversions form in polar regions when the sun doesn't rise for weeks or months, and these are sources of cold waves. In warmer places, inversions can develop overnight. Inversions also form where air from aloft is sinking to create surface high pressure. Inversions sometimes form caps that keep warm air from rising, preventing thunderstorm development. When rising air finally breaks such an inversion, the hot air that has been bottled up can quickly rise to form severe thunderstorms.

Blue Sky

Anyone who isn't color-blind and who looks at the sky knows it's blue. But why? The sky's blue has baffled some of the world's best minds, from the ancient Greeks to 19th-century physicists.

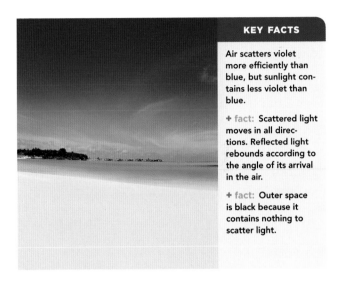

KEY FACTS

Air scatters violet more efficiently than blue, but sunlight contains less violet than blue.

+ fact: Scattered light moves in all directions. Reflected light rebounds according to the angle of its arrival in the air.

+ fact: Outer space is black because it contains nothing to scatter light.

From Aristotle to Leonardo da Vinci and Isaac Newton, the greatest minds of science throughout world history have tried to explain why the sky is blue. Many ideas included reflection of one kind or another. Finally the British physicist John William Strutt, usually referred to as Lord Rayleigh, solved the puzzle in the 1870s. Since Newton, it had been known that sunlight is composed of all colors, which can be split apart by a prism. Lord Rayleigh suggested that some colors in light scatter more readily than others. Blue scatters the most; hence, the sky looks blue, except around sunrise and sunset.

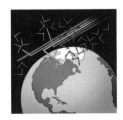

||||||||||||||||||||||||||||||||||||||||||||||||||||||||||||||||||||||||||||||||

Mirages

In meteorological parlance, a mirage is not a hallucination—it is an optical distortion caused by atmospheric conditions. In fact, you can photograph a mirage, as many people have.

KEY FACTS

Outside of polar regions, superior mirages are much less common but are more stable than inferior mirages.

+ fact: In May 1909, a superior mirage in Greenland showed explorer Donald B. MacMillan land that was 200 mi (320 km) away.

+ fact: Because hot air rises, inferior mirages are unstable and may distort images.

Mirages are caused when layers of air at different temperatures bend light in various ways, distorting an apparent object into an image that does not correspond with physical reality. The greater the temperature differences, the more striking the mirage. Air near the ground that is warmer than air higher can create an "inferior mirage," with objects appearing lower than they really are. For instance, the sky might appear as a pool of water in the desert. A thermal inversion—air near the ground that is colder than air higher—can create a "superior mirage," with objects appearing higher than they are. Striking superior mirages occur especially in the polar regions, including some that show objects that are below the horizon to the viewer's eye.

Fata Morgana

A fata morgana is a complex mirage with elements both compressed and stretched, both inverted and right side up, combining into visions that change quickly.

KEY FACTS

Fata morganas are named for Morgan le Fay, the shape-shifting sorceress of the King Arthur legends.

+ fact: In 1906 explorer Robert Peary named land he saw "Crocker Land." It was a fata morgana.

+ fact: A famous fata morgana is the *Flying Dutchman*, a ghost frigate doomed to sail forever, according to folklore.

Steep thermal inversions with warm air over cold water, cold air, or polar ice help create the atmospheric ducts needed to evoke a fata morgana mirage. An atmospheric duct is a layer in the lower atmosphere that guides light along Earth's curvature. The components of a fata morgana can shift between being inferior and superior mirages. Some fata morganas create multiple images, alternately expanded and compressed vertically.

At times fata morganas appear to be buildings of a city or appear as the hills of an island where none exists. Over the years, fata morganas have led polar explorers to map islands or other lands that don't exist. Numerous reports of ghost ships, sometimes in the air, are likely the results of these illusions.

Thunderstorm Safety

An estimated 100,000 thunderstorms hit the United States yearly. Ten percent of thunderstorms are severe—with winds of 58 mph (93 kph) or faster, large hailstones, or a tornado.

KEY FACTS

When thunderstorms are likely, make sure to stay near shelter in case a storm develops.

+ fact: A severe thunderstorm watch means severe thunderstorms are possible; you should be ready to take shelter.

+ fact: A severe thunderstorm warning means a severe thunderstorm has been spotted; you should take shelter.

Lightning is the big danger in all thunderstorms. Severe thunderstorms add the danger of winds that can topple trees and send debris flying. A sturdy building is the best shelter against both. Your best defense is not being caught far from safe shelter—hiking up a mountain, two hours or more away from safety, for instance—when a thunderstorm hits. Although forecasters can give advance warning about hurricanes and winter storms, they can rarely predict when and where a thunderstorm will hit more than about a half hour ahead. They can, however, pin down general areas where thunderstorms are likely to occur hours ahead of time. Use these general alerts to plan time outdoors to ensure that you won't be caught in the open.

Lightning Safety

Lightning is one of the top three weather killers most years in the United States. If you are anywhere outdoors when you hear thunder or see a lighting flash, lightning could hit you.

KEY FACTS

If you see lightning or hear thunder, no matter how far away, immediately take shelter.

+ fact: Enclosed buildings with electrical wiring and plumbing or enclosed metal vehicles are the best shelters.

+ fact: If lightning catches you outdoors, don't squat or lie on the ground and don't hide under a tree. Run for shelter as fast as you can.

The lightning to be concerned about is a powerful but very brief electrical current seeking a path to the ground with the least resistance. To avoid death or injury, you need to avoid being that easiest path to the ground that it is seeking. When you are inside an enclosed building with electrical service and plumbing, lightning will find the building's wires or pipes to be a better path to the ground. But stay away from water and from anything plugged in, including a telephone with a wire, when you are inside. (A cell phone is safe.) An enclosed vehicle is safe because electricity goes through the metal and to the ground, but a strong lightning strike could blow out the tires.

Heat Exhaustion and Heatstroke

High temperatures and humidity upset the body's systems for regulating temperature. Perspiration is the body's natural cooler, but humidity hinders evaporation, making you hotter.

KEY FACTS

Heatstroke, also called sunstroke, is a medical emergency worth a 911 call.

+ fact: The National Weather Service Heat Index combines temperature and humidity for an "apparent temperature."

+ fact: Many cities have cooling centers where the elderly and others endangered by heat can relax in air-conditioned places.

The dangers presented by extreme heat and humidity are different for healthy men and women than for the elderly and people in ill health who don't have air-conditioning. If you know someone in this latter category, checking on them through a heat spell could be a lifesaver. For those in good health, the dangers arise when a person is so focused on a workout or sport that signs of trouble, such as cramps or thirst, are ignored. Heat exhaustion with heavy sweating, weakness, and pale, clammy skin is serious. Victims should get out of the sun—into air- conditioning if possible—and sip water. Heatstroke with a high body temperature could be next, leading even to unconsciousness. This would be a medical emergency.

Tornado Safety

Tornadoes are the strongest storms on Earth, but they are small in reach and relatively rare, with the strongest ones extremely rare. It's still a good idea to know what to do if one threatens you.

KEY FACTS

Flying debris is a tornado's greatest danger; avoiding it should be your main safety goal.

+ fact: Don't waste time opening windows as a tornado approaches; flying debris will do it for you.

+ fact: Don't even think of sheltering under a highway overpass; wind squeezing through makes it a debris-laden wind tunnel.

Because a tornado's path cannot be predicted until it is on the ground, you and your family need to have a tornado plan. You could even conduct a tornado drill, as schools do. Because your goal is to avoid flying debris, you should take shelter in a low room with no windows. A windowless basement under a strong workbench or table offers the best protection. In a high-rise building, the interior stairway is the best shelter. Forget the elevator—tornadoes bring power failures. Many schools and shopping centers on the Great Plains, where tornadoes are more prevalent, have tornado shelters marked with signs. Walk-in coolers have saved many people when tornados hit restaurants or convenience stores. If a tornado threatens, you should seek shelter.

Hurricane Safety

Two good rules for responding when a hurricane threatens your home or where you are staying are: Run from the water and hide from the wind. To do so, you need to know the flood danger.

KEY FACTS

Water is the biggest hurricane killer: both the water that a storm pushes ashore and the flash floods it can create inland.

+ fact: Wind can destroy a well-built house if the windows are not protected against flying debris.

+ fact: You need to check flood maps to see whether a hurricane could flood your home.

Over the centuries and around the world, hurricanes and tropical cyclones have killed more people with water than with wind. Usually, the highest death tolls are from flash floods from downpours dumped by dying storms far inland. If inundation maps show that your home is well clear of any possible surge, you can think about hiding from the wind at home. But, as Hurricane Andrew in 1992 proved in South Florida—the region of the United States where hurricanes are most likely to hit—expensive homes were not necessarily built to withstand storms. If you expect a need to evacuate, plan where you'll go and what you'll take before hurricane season begins. You should have storm shutters or plywood window covers ready before hurricane season begins.

Cold Weather Safety

Cold weather brings two unique health threats: frostbite (freezing of tissue such as your fingers) and hypothermia (a lowering of your body's core temperature).

KEY FACTS

U.S. Antarctic Program survival schools stress staying hydrated to help avoid hypothermia and frostbite.

+ fact: The U.S. National Weather Service and Environment Canada used wind-tunnel tests with volunteers to develop windchill charts.

+ fact: Hypothermia can occur at temperatures above 40°F (4.4°C) if a victim is wet.

Frostbite can result in lost tissue but is not life threatening unless it is untreated and leads to gangrene. Hypothermia is always life threatening if not stopped in time. Windchill figures can alert you to the danger of both. Windchill does not change the temperature. If the temperature is above freezing with the windchill below freezing, your fingers and toes cannot freeze.

Nevertheless, a frigid windchill means wind is carrying warmth away from your body faster than in calm air. This can speed hypothermia, when your body's core temperature falls below 95°F (35°C). First aid for hypothermia includes removing wet clothing and carefully warming a victim without burning him or her. Mental confusion can be a symptom of hypothermia.

Winter Storm Safety

If a winter storm traps you at home or in your car, be prepared to stay warm to avoid hypothermia. Carbon monoxide poisoning is a major winter storm danger.

KEY FACTS

Roughly 70 percent of deaths related to ice and snow occur in vehicles.

+ fact: A winter storm watch means you should prepare for snow or ice that closes roads and interrupts electric power.

+ fact: About 50 percent of those who die from hypothermia are over age 60.

A winter storm watch should signal you to stock up on food, water, prescription medications, and other things you will need if you find yourself trapped at home with roads closed by ice or snow and possibly having no electrical power for a few days. These threats are worse in the South, where snow and ice are uncommon and people are less well prepared.

Anything that burns fuel—a generator, a charcoal grill, or a backpacking stove—produces carbon monoxide, so be sure to use these in ventilated places. The fumes are toxic. If you must go anywhere in a car, you should be dressed to survive for a few hours in the conditions outside, so that if you slide off the road or find yourself otherwise immobilized, you can survive the cold.

||||||||||||||||||||||||||||||||||||||||||||||||||||||||||||||||||||||||||||||||

Flood Safety

The main flood danger, especially in flash floods, is drowning when trying to walk or drive into floodwaters. The danger continues after waters recede; bacterial contamination remains.

KEY FACTS

You shouldn't wade in floodwater if the water is moving faster than you can walk, or if you cannot see the bottom.

+ fact: A mere 12 to 18 in (30 to 46 cm) of water is enough to lift and carry a car downstream with a good chance of it rolling over.

+ fact: More than half of those killed in floods are inside vehicles.

An essential element of flood safety is keeping healthy after a flood. When you clean up, you may not want to think about what was in the water that soaked everything, but you must think about it enough to protect yourself from diseases and hazardous chemicals. If possible, find out what could have been in the floodwater. Your hepatitis A and tetanus shots should be current. The Federal Emergency Management Agency recommends wearing boots for flood cleanup and having bleach and water to decontaminate them before getting into your car or going into your home or garage. Also, remember that floods can seriously weaken buildings, so be aware of structural dangers as well. Flooded buildings can harbor venomous snakes.

||||||||||||||||||||||||||||||||||||||||||||||||||||||||||||||||||||||||||||||||||||||||||

Surface Weather Observations

Weather data such as temperature, atmospheric pressure, wind speed, and wind direction are raw materials for weather forecasts and the ground truth used to check forecast accuracy.

KEY FACTS

All of the world's weather stations use Coordinated Universal Time (formerly Greenwich [mean] time) for observation times.

+ fact: Weather averages for locations are based on 30 years of observations, updated every 10 years.

+ fact: Almost all U.S. weather observations are collected and transmitted automatically.

As the computers used to produce weather forecasts become more powerful, they can handle more and more data. Data are being collected and fed into the National Weather Service (NWS) network not only from traditional weather stations but also from automated stations at numerous small airports and locations operated by state, local, and private highway operators. Electronic devices that sense data such as atmospheric pressure make automated stations possible. In addition to traditional observations, the NWS receives data including water levels in streams, dryness of woodland areas, and soil temperatures and moisture levels.

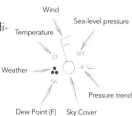

|||||||||||||||||||||||||||||||||||||||||||||||||||||||||||||||||||||||||||||||||||

Aviation Weather

Aviation is extremely weather dependent, hence the effort that the Canadian Weather Office and the U.S. National Weather Service put into collecting data for aviation forecasts.

KEY FACTS

Ceiling is the height above ground of the lowest level of clouds covering more than six-tenths of the sky.

+ fact: **Sky condition refers to the heights of layers of clouds and how much sky each layer covers.**

+ fact: **Pilots use local altimeter readings to adjust their altimeters for the airport's air pressure.**

Automated stations at airports provide all sorts of information essential to pilots. The height of the cloud ceiling and current visibility are essential elements in flying and air traffic management. Pilots normally point into the wind for takeoff and landing, so wind speed and direction are necessary knowledge. If the wind is not blowing directly down a runway, pilots prefer to use the runway that is nearest to pointing into the wind. Pilots flying into small airports can use a special radio frequency to hear the airport's automated weather report. The U.S. National Weather Service produces most U.S. aviation forecasts. The Aviation Weather Center in Kansas City supplies nationwide predictions, and local NWS offices make forecasts for airports. Some airlines employ forecasters.

Measuring Snow

Scientists are working on high-tech instruments to measure
the amount of snow that falls, but for now, plywood left on the
ground and rulers are still the best way to track snowfall.

KEY FACTS

To be considered measurable, at least 0.1 in
(0.25 cm) of snow has
to fall; less is reported
as a "trace."

+ fact: With powder
snow, approximately
20 in (50 cm) amounts
to an inch of water.

+ fact: In a heavy, wet
snow, only 5 in (13 cm)
of snow may amount
to an inch of water.

National Weather Service volunteer observers use a
"snowboard"—a 16-by-16-inch (41 cm) piece of plywood on the ground in a place without drifts or bare spots
as snow falls. Each hour, the volunteer uses a ruler marked
in tenths of an inch to measure the snow and then brushes
the board clean. Another board that is not brushed off
measures the snow on the ground after natural settling
and melting. In the western mountains, the U.S. Natural
Resources Conservation Service uses automated instruments that measure the weight of snow and then convert
it into water content. That information helps forecasters to
predict water flows in western rivers when the snow melts.
Melting snow is also an important source of soil moisture
for farmers.

Upper Air Weather Observations

Data about winds, temperatures, humidity, and other atmospheric properties measured as high as 100,000 feet (30,000 m) above Earth are vital for making today's forecasts.

KEY FACTS

Radiosondes rise until the balloon bursts, above 100,000 ft (30,000 m); tiny parachutes lower them to the ground.

+ fact: If you find a radiosonde, directions on the side tell how to return it.

+ fact: From 1898 to 1933, the Weather Bureau used kites to collect data up to 10,000 ft (3,000 m).

Since the 1940s, basic upper air data have come from weather balloons carrying radiosondes, small boxes that collect and radio back the data twice a day. Approximately 800 global weather stations launch balloons once or twice a day. Extra balloons are launched when more data are needed on a storm. The main supplement to balloon data is automated reports that many airliners send every few minutes measuring temperatures, wind speeds, and wind directions. When all U.S. airline flights were grounded September 11–13, 2001, the accuracy of forecasts dropped significantly. Forecasts for three hours ahead were only as accurate as 12-day predictions using constant airline data. The forecasts most affected were those especially intended for aviation, but others were also less accurate.

High-Altitude Turbulence

Although turbulence isn't likely to bring down one of today's airliners, it regularly causes injuries to passengers en route. Researchers are seeking ways to warn pilots of turbulence.

KEY FACTS

Most lower-altitude severe turbulence is in or near clouds; pilots know which clouds to avoid.

+ fact: **FAA statistics show that passengers not wearing seat belts account for 98 percent of turbulence injuries.**

+ fact: **High-altitude turbulence encounters are mostly in clear air with no warning.**

CLEAR AIR TURBULENCE (CAT) RISK
MEDIUM
06HR FCST BASED ON 12Z NAM FEB 27, 2013 -

Most high-altitude turbulence is in or near jet-stream winds with few clouds. Because radar tracks by sensing cloud water drops or ice crystals, turbulence outside of clouds is invisible to an airliner's radar. The best forecasters can do now is predict where turbulence is likely to occur. An airplane's turbulence encounter is a good detector for other airplanes, and pilots and air traffic controllers exchange real-time turbulence information via radio. Researchers are developing a LIDAR (a radar that uses light instead of microwaves) for airplanes, which shows promise for spotting turbulence. Others are testing ways to use data from ground-based Doppler radars, which collect more data than airliners' radars, to spot high-altitude turbulence.

Weather Research Airplanes

Unlike many other scientists, meteorologists can get inside the phenomena they study. Since weather extends to the edge of space, scientists need aircraft to examine the weather in full.

KEY FACTS

NOAA's two WP-3D hurricane hunters began flying into hurricanes in 1977 and are still at it.

+ fact: In 1987, NASA's ER-2, based in Chile, collected Antarctic ozone hole data.

+ fact: In 2012, NASA's Global Hawk, a large unmanned airplane, made the first of many planned flights observing hurricanes from above.

Weather balloons collect needed data, but to study the weather scientists must be able to say: "What's that? Let's take a look." Research flights into hurricanes grew out of the reconnaissance flights by the U.S. military during World War II. Meteorologists on some flights learned new things about hurricanes and saw the value of studying storms from airplanes. This has led to today's research fleet, which includes NASA's ER-2, a civilian version of the U-2 spy plane; two Gulfstream business jets equipped as flying research labs; and NOAA's two WP-3Ds, which are best known for hurricane flights but have helped scientists investigate weather phenomena globally, including El Niño, winter storms, ocean winds, Great Plains thunderstorms, and low-level jet streams.

Tornado Chasing

Since the 1970s, scientists have realized that the only way to improve tornado forecasts is to collect extensive data on what happens inside the supercells that spawn the strongest twisters.

KEY FACTS

VORTEX-1 produced the first full documentation of the life cycle of a tornado.

+ fact: The worst tornado in U.S. history happened in 1925, killing 695 people in Missouri, Illinois, and Indiana.

+ fact: A person is more likely to fall off a cliff or contract leprosy than be killed by a tornado.

Tornado researchers began using portable Doppler radar devices in 1995 to collect unprecedented close-up views of tornadic supercells. VORTEX (Verification of the Origins of Rotation in Tornadoes Experiment) is the largest tornado research project ever, designed to study how, when, and why tornadoes form. In 1994–95, 18 vehicles collected data as part of VORTEX-1; in 2009–10, roughly 100 men and women in 40 vehicles collected data from 11 supercells as part of VORTEX-2. The goal of these storm chases was to find changes inside supercells that could be detected, measured, and used in the future as indicators that a strong tornado is likely to form. VORTEX-2 scientists will be studying data and presenting analyses for another decade.

Weather Radar

Radar transmitters emit microwaves that objects such as raindrops scatter, some back to the radar. Computers convert the signals into information such as precipitation location.

The U.S. and the United Kingdom developed radar during World War II to detect and track enemy ships and aircraft. When researchers encountered interference caused by precipitation—rain or snow—they began applying radar to track weather phenomena as well. The U.S. National Weather Service (NWS) completed its first nationwide radar network (NEXRAD) in 1967, and radar quickly became important for both forecasters and researchers. Today, radar meteorology is a separate branch of the science. In 2012, NWS finished updating all its current radars to dual polarization, which supplies more data about the nature of precipitation.

Weather Forecasting

Computerized predictions are the core of all of today's professional weather forecasts. As computers have gained power and speed since the 1950s, predictions have improved.

KEY FACTS

A 40 percent chance of rain means that any place in the area has a 40 percent chance of at least 0.01 in (0.25 mm).

+ fact: "Isolated showers" should affect 20 percent or less of an area; "scattered showers," 30–50 percent; "numerous showers," 60–70 percent.

+ fact: Wording such as "rain today" means that more than 80 percent of an area will be affected.

Forecasts begin with weather data from around the world flowing into the National Weather Service (NWS) National Centers for Environmental Prediction in College Park, Maryland. Supercomputers use the data to run several "models" and search for patterns. These are computer programs that use equations of fluid dynamics and thermodynamics to predict weather around the world, with more detailed forecasts for all of the United States. These are sent as maps and data that local NWS offices and other meteorologists use as starting points for their predictions. The results of different models enable forecasters to get what amount to second, or even third, opinions on what's likely to happen. These products are available on the Internet for anyone to use.

Weather Satellites

Weather satellites are such a part of our lives today that we're no longer amazed by their stunning images, such as of hurricanes. They collect other data as well as taking pictures.

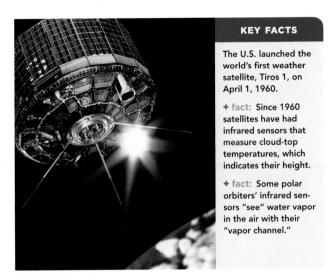

KEY FACTS

The U.S. launched the world's first weather satellite, Tiros 1, on April 1, 1960.

+ fact: Since 1960 satellites have had infrared sensors that measure cloud-top temperatures, which indicates their height.

+ fact: Some polar orbiters' infrared sensors "see" water vapor in the air with their "vapor channel."

Almost all the satellite images you see come from geostationary satellites, which orbit 22,238 miles (35,788 km) above the Equator. At this altitude their orbital speed matches Earth's rotation, keeping them above the same spot. They scan an entire disk of Earth. The United States has two of these, which with similar satellites of other nations give global coverage.

Polar orbiters circle Earth from north to south and back 540 miles (869 km) high. Their closer view allows them to collect more detailed atmospheric data. For example, one polar orbiter's cloud-top temperature sensor detects changes 540 miles below—equivalent to detecting whether a lightbulb 22.6 miles (36 km) away is 100 watts or 101.6 watts.

Weather Radio

Some weather warnings, such as those for tornadoes and flash floods, require immediate action. The consequences of missing a warning could be dire.

KEY FACTS

The NWS began Weather Radio in 1967. From then until the 1990s, local meteorologists recorded on tape.

+ fact: In the late 1990s a text-to-computer system using "Paul" was introduced, but many didn't like his voice.

+ fact: The text-to-voice system introduced in 2000 has "Donna," "Tom," and a Spanish voice, "Javier."

All National Weather Service (NWS) offices broadcast warnings on NOAA Weather Radio, which requires special receivers to hear. The necessary radios, which pick up the seven VHF frequencies used for weather radio, are available at most stores that sell electronics. Many of these radios can also be used as ordinary radios. Most have a feature that will automatically turn the radio on and sound an alarm when a warning is broadcast.

Newer weather radios have Specific Area Message Encoding (SAME), which allows those interested to program the radio to turn on and sound the alarm only for warnings for an area that is specified. This setting will exclude warnings for other parts of the region the local NWS office covers.

Ocean Observations

Weather doesn't begin at the ocean's edge. Forecasters need data from along the coast and far out at sea to make forecasts. Automated buoys and coastal stations meet this need.

KEY FACTS

The U.S. maintains Pacific Ocean buoys collecting data to track El Niño.

+ fact: Hurricane Sandy in 2012 hit a New York Harbor data buoy with a record 32.5-ft (10 m) wave.

+ fact: A 141 mph (226 kph) wind at the Fowey Rocks C-MAN station was the highest recorded when Hurricane Andrew hit Dade County, Florida, in 1982.

The short towers and moored buoys marked as belonging to NOAA are supplying weather data NWS forecasters said they required, as in the 1980s. The U.S. Coast Guard was automating lighthouses, whose keepers were also weather observers. The NWS set up its National Data Buoy Center to maintain the Coastal-Marine Automated Network (C-MAN) stations along the U.S. coast as well as buoys moored in the water to collect data. When a hurricane or extratropical cyclone is battering the shore, forecasters and the public turn to reports from these stations to see how bad the storm is. Even more important, the stations also supply vital information on average winds and waves as well as extreme events in the same way weather stations on land supply the climate data needed for planning.

Short-term Forecasts

A general rule in meteorology is that the further into the future a weather forecast projects, the higher are the odds that the forecast will not be accurate.

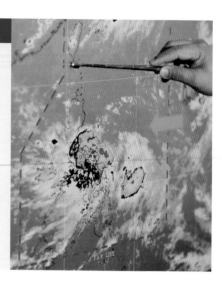

The U.S. National Weather Service (NWS) and the Canadian Weather Office, along with many private forecasters, regularly produce day-to-day forecasts 10 days ahead. In general, it is wisest not to make any important decisions based on a forecast for more than two or three days into the future. The atmosphere is an extremely complex system in which minor differences in the present can have major consequences in the near future. Furthermore, the atmosphere is chaotic, with random changes that no model or computer can predict accurately. When a forecast contains a percentage—"a 40 percent chance of rain," for instance—the meteorologist has calculated both physical likelihood and confidence in the prediction.

Long-term Forecasts

The NWS Climate Prediction Center produces outlooks for short and long periods: from the next 6 to 14 days to the 3-month period ending 12 months ahead.

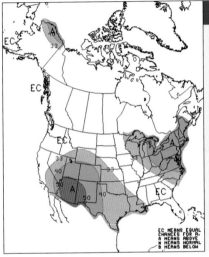

EC MEANS EQUAL
CHANCES FOR A.
A MEANS ABOVE
N MEANS NORMAL
B MEANS BELOW

KEY FACTS

The National Weather Service says outlooks for temperatures are most accurate in late winter and late summer.

+ fact: All precipitation outlooks are less accurate than those for temperatures.

+ fact: A strong El Niño makes the precipitation outlook as likely to be correct as some temperature forecasts.

Weather outlooks are intended for rather sophisticated users who are comfortable with probabilities. All outlooks calculate average temperatures over month-long or three-month periods. They will never be specific enough to select a fall weekend for a college homecoming, but they will have general information one could use to estimate fuel oil needs through the period. Still, it's a gamble: If the long-term forecast calls for a cold winter, you can contract to buy oil for the season at a low but fixed price. But if the winter turns out to be warmer than predicted, the fuel costs could drop below the total price you paid. Nevertheless, by using long-term forecasts, you would be like a professional poker player who loses occasionally but wins more often.

Weather Watches

The terms "watch" and "warning" for potentially dangerous weather may sound somewhat the same, yet they have distinctly different meanings.

The U.S. National Weather Service (NWS) and Canada's Weather Office issue a weather watch when forecasters see a chance that a dangerous event will occur but do not yet consider it a sure thing. A given locale will be put under storm watch, for instance, when the storm is still far enough away not to pose an immediate threat. What you should do when you hear a storm watch depends on the kind of event. A tornado could happen an hour or so after NWS issues a watch. A hurricane could arrive 48 hours after the watch begins. Depending on the kind of event, it can mean that you should stay alert and be ready to act, or it can mean that you should prepare for an event that could greatly impact your daily life, such as a hurricane or winter storm.

Weather Warnings

A weather warning indicates imminent danger. When it is issued, you should already have used the weather watch period to prepare to keep you and your family safe from the hazard.

KEY FACTS

Each weather warning includes specific advice for the wisest steps to take for safety.

+ fact: A flash-flood warning means leave quickly if you're in a location subject to flash floods.

+ fact: A red flag warning means conditions are right for wildfires to start and spread rapidly, so great care must be taken and no open fires should be lit.

A weather warning means dangerous conditions are occurring or will occur soon. NWS and Canada's Weather Office consider a warning to indicate a threat to life or property. Ideally, you heard the watch and already planned what to do in response. Tornado warnings often advise people to take shelter in a place safe from flying debris. When a winter storm warning is in place, you should stay off the road, remaining safe in your home or elsewhere with the supplies you'll need for a day or two. Hurricane warnings are issued approximately 36 hours before the brunt of the storm is expected, because responses to an oncoming hurricane are more complex and take more time. You should evacuate if you're in a possible flood zone or a home that won't withstand high winds.

Extreme Weather Safety
A Guide to Emergency Preparedness

A hurricane is coming. Should you leave home or stay put? At home, are you better off upstairs or downstairs? How do you access local alerts? Many face those questions in the heat of the moment, but it's best to think the answers through carefully, long before a storm. The checklists in the following section of this book offer a practical guide to weather safety. Start planning and preparing—now.

Get Ready

Set up a meeting with all members of your household to talk about preparation and response to weather emergencies. Alert everyone to the types of problems that may arise. Meeting places need to be chosen—one nearby in case of, say, a fire. And one in a different area in case you need to evacuate your home. Identify the location of a designated local shelter. It's also wise to have emergency contacts saved on your mobile phones and identified as ICE, or "in case of emergency." Emergency responders are trained to look for these labels on mobile phones. Assign tasks for each member of the household to ensure a well-organized, swift, and safe response to disasters. For example, if there is a flood, who's in charge of moving furniture to a higher, drier place? Turning off the power? What about pets—who is minding them? If a heat wave hits, can elderly family members care for themselves? If not, who will look in on them?

We seem to be getting slammed harder and more frequently by weather disasters. The news is filled with catastrophic hurricanes and typhoons, and in many places, summers are hotter or winters are colder. Stay informed about inclement weather in your area and make an emergency kit. Good preparation will allow you to maintain control over your emotions when a disaster hits. Staying calm and focused are critical practices that every emergency responder knows can make the difference between life and death. With more extreme weather events occurring now than in the past, learning how to prepare and survive is—like it or not—an integral part of life in the 21st century.

Thunderstorm Safety

How to Prepare

What To Do

☑ Follow the 30/30 Lightning Safety Rule: When you see lightning, start counting. If you hear thunder before you count to 30, head indoors—and stay indoors for 30 minutes until you hear no more thunder.

☑ Close all windows and doors. Also, close all shutters, blinds, shades, or curtains.

☑ Unplug sensitive or electrical equipment and appliances of which you are not in immediate need.

☑ Choose a gathering spot inside your home that is away from windows, skylights, and glass doors. Inform all household members of the plan.

☑ Tie down and/or fasten objects outside your home that might blow away and cause damage.

☑ Inspect shelters for pets or outdoor animals; have a plan to bring pets inside if needed.

☑ If you are hiking or camping, have a plan in case a storm comes. Find shelter options, and make sure everyone in your party knows where to go. If you plan to go outback camping, make sure thunderstorms aren't forecast.

What Not To Do

☑ Do not let loose items or trash pile up outside your house. Also, keep trees trimmed and healthy. These can fall or blow in high storm winds and cause serious injury and/or property damage.

☑ Do not install lightning rods without first consulting your local fire department to ensure they abide by fire codes.

☑ Do not plan outdoors activities if a storm watch is in effect.

☑ Do not ignore signs of an approaching thunderstorm. The storm doesn't have to be overhead in order for you to be struck. Lightning can travel 5 to 10 miles and strike the ground with blue sky overhead.

How to Stay Safe

What To Do

☑ Take precautions even if a storm is in the distance. Lightning strikes travel well beyond the rain cloud.

☑ If you are driving a vehicle, exit the road and park. Remain in your vehicle and turn on the emergency flashers until the storm ends. Do not drive through flooded areas.

☑ If you are on foot, seek shelter in the nearest and sturdiest building. Stay away from tall objects such as trees or towers or poles.

☑ Tents do not offer protection from lightning. If you are camping, seek out sturdier structures if possible or your vehicle.

☑ Stay away from water and wet items. A lightning strike far away can travel long distances via water.

☑ If you are in a small boat, get to shore as quickly as possible. Large boats with cabins, especially those equipped with lightning protection systems, are relatively safe, according to the National Oceanic and Atmospheric Administration (NOAA).

☑ If lightning has struck someone administer CPR if needed and call for medical assistance as soon as possible. Lightning can cause heart attacks.

☑ Even after rain subsides, stay alert for flood warnings.

What Not To Do

☑ If caught outdoors, do not lie on the ground. Most deaths occur when lightning strikes nearby and spreads through the ground.

☑ Do not use corded phones or devices. Instead operate wireless phones not connected to a wall outlet.

☑ Do not touch plumbing. That means no washing your hands or doing laundry. Plumbing and bathroom fixtures conduct electricity.

☑ Do not touch metal or other surfaces that likely conduct electricity, especially if inside a vehicle.

☑ Do not worry about touching a person who has been struck by lighting; no shock will occur.

Drought Safety

How to Prepare

What To Do

☑ Check your house for leaks, and repair any dripping faucets. A drip a second wastes more than 3,000 gallons of water a year.

☑ Consider buying low-flow faucets, shower heads, and toilets. These appliances may be pricey up front, but they can decrease your freshwater use and lower water bills over the long run.

☑ Plant drought-tolerant vegetation and mulch the garden to hold moisture in soil. Some plants, such as cacti and low-water grasses, can cut as much as two-thirds of the water you might use for thirstier plants. Also, some water utility companies offer incentives and rebates for you to plant water-wise plants.

☑ Always water the landscape in the morning or evening, when temperatures are cooler and water doesn't evaporate as quickly. Irrigate in multiple sessions for shorter lengths of time and position a rotating spigot so it isn't needlessly spraying paved areas to avoid runoff. Invest in soaking hoses rather than sprinklers.

☑ In case of a heat wave or power outage keep coolers in the house and frozen bottles of water in the freezer.

☑ Properly insulate your house. Check weather stripping on doors and windows, ensure that window air conditioners fit snugly, and hang shades on windows in direct sunlight.

What Not To Do

☑ Do not waste water by pouring it down the drain. There may be another use for it, such as cleaning or watering plants.

☑ Don't use your kitchen sink disposal as a garbage bin. Disposals require a lot of water to operate.

☑ Do not let your garden hose run; install a shutoff nozzle. An unrestricted garden hose can use water at a rate of as much as 12 gallons a minute.

☑ If you have a pool, do not leave it uncovered.

☑ Do not overwater your garden. About half of the water used outdoors goes to waste from evaporation or runoff. Watering once or twice a week is sufficient.

How to Stay Safe

What To Do

☑ Wash vegetables in a large bowl or dish instead of with running tap water.

☑ Keep drinking water in the refrigerator rather than having the tap run for cool water.

☑ Hand-wash dishes by filling two containers—one for cleaning with soapy water and another for rinsing with clear water.

☑ Set family time limits for showers.

☑ Allow your lawn to be sacrificed in times of extreme drought to preserve trees and large shrubs.

☑ During rising temperatures look out for signs your body is overheating. These include nausea, vomiting, headaches, dizziness, weakness, and confusion. If your pets stay outside, provide cool water and shade.

☑ Stay alert for news of wildfires and prepare an evacuation plan for your household, especially if you live in a fire-prone area.

☑ If you encounter a dust storm, use a mask or piece of fabric to cover your nose and mouth. Wrap as much of your skin in clothing as possible to protect it against blowing dirt and debris. If you are driving, pull completely off the roadway, turn off all lights, and wait inside the vehicle.

What Not To Do

☑ Do not waste tap water that flows as you wait for it to warm. Heat water on the stove or in a microwave.

☑ Do not waste water on yards or car washing during heat emergencies.

☑ Do not let the water run as you brush your teeth, wash your face, or shave, and do not flush the toilet more than you must.

☑ Do not take baths. They can use three times as much water as the average shower.

☑ During rising temperatures do not keep lights on or run high energy-consuming appliances during the hottest part of the day. These not only increase heat inside your home, but also strain the electric grid and present a greater likelihood of power outage.

Tornado Safety

How to Prepare

What To Do

☑ Listen for tornado warnings and weather reports. Remember that a "watch" means threatening conditions, whereas a "warning" means tornadoes in the area.

☑ Identify ahead of time your best source for weather information if you live in a tornado-prone area. Prepare for no power and know how you will get info even without it and how to connect with family members during and after a tornado.

☑ Learn to know the weather warning signs of tornadoes: a dark, greenish sky; a wall cloud—dark, low, isolated thunder cloud; a loud, insistent roar; clouds of debris; large hailstones; and, of course, a funnel cloud forming up under a thunderstorm cloud.

What Not To Do

☑ If possible, do not remain in a mobile home if a tornado watch has been issued. Seek sturdier shelter nearby immediately.

☑ Do not leave the house if a tornado watch has been issued.

☑ Do not leave any outdoor items such as grills, furniture, trash cans, or potted plants outdoors around your house. These items can get swept up and become flying weapons that cause personal and property hazards.

☑ Do not assume that no visible funnel cloud means no tornado is coming. Often the swirling winds are not visible until they pick up dirt and debris.

How to Stay Safe

What To Do

☑ Go to your safe room in the basement or an interior room on the lowest floor. Consider a bathroom, a closet without windows, or a closet under the stairs.

☑ Try to put as many walls as possible between you and the outside.

☑ Leave a mobile home immediately and go to a more sound building or a designated shelter.

☑ Put an infant into a car seat for added protection indoors, but don't waste time running out to the car to get the seat if a warning has already been issued.

☑ Wear sturdy shoes so you can walk for a long distance or run if you are forced from your location. Gather your prescription medications, wallet, and keys only if you have time.

☑ If you are caught outdoors, find a ditch or sloping area below roadway level. Lie down and cover your head with your hands.

☑ In the aftermath, watch where you step, both inside and outdoors. Half of tornado-related injuries are suffered during rescue attempts, cleanup, and other post-tornado activities. Nearly one-third of those injuries come from stepping on nails.

What Not To Do

☑ Do not go anywhere near downed power lines. Even objects near downed power lines can be dangerous, and current can travel through water or cement.

☑ Do not wait until you see a tornado before you take cautionary measures.

☑ Do not take shelter underneath an overpass or bridge. You are much safer finding a low, flat location.

☑ Do not open any windows no matter what type of building or structure you are in. It is a myth that open windows equalize the pressure and can prevent your house from exploding.

Hurricane Safety

How to Prepare

What To Do

☑ Keep an adequate supply of bottled water in a safe place. Water may not be available for days. Before a hurricane, fill sinks, tubs, and other large containers.

☑ Put together a plan on how to best secure your property, including how to cover windows and better fasten your roof to its frame.

☑ Do not tempt timing. Trust public announcements and safety directions, even if they seem conservative. Evacuate if you are told to do so by officials, and follow their instructions.

☑ Find out if your area has community evacuation routes.

☑ If you live in a high-rise building, determine a place to go on a lower floor—experts recommend below the 10th floor.

☑ Become aware of any bodies of water close by, including human-made dams and levees, that could be affected by a hurricane or its accompanying storm surge.

☑ Check trees and shrubs around your home to ensure they are well trimmed and wind resistant.

☑ Keep all gutters and drains clean and clear.

☑ Have a plan and a place to store outdoor furniture and loose items such as grills and garbage cans.

What Not To Do

☑ Do not keep all appliances plugged in if a storm is approaching. Only leave necessary electronics plugged in.

☑ Do not let your vehicle's fuel tank dip too low. Keep a full tank in case you have to evacuate.

☑ Do not leave your windows exposed. If you don't have storm shutters, board windows with plywood.

☑ Do not forget to detach the propane tank for your barbecue grill before securing the grill or bringing it under cover.

How to Stay Safe

What To Do

☑ Keep curtains and blinds closed. These can act as added protection from flying debris.

☑ Keep doors to the outside closed and locked.

☑ Stay inside and in an interior room, preferably in the basement or on the ground floor. It's better to take refuge in smaller rooms in the center of your home. A closet or hallway on the lowest level can provide safety.

☑ Remember that the eye of the hurricane is calm and therefore deceptive; it may simply mean the storm is halfway over. Stay safe until you are sure the storm has passed.

☑ Look for flooding, and stay off flooded roads and washed-out bridges.

☑ Be alert for tornadoes; hurricanes can sometimes produce these as a by-product of their severity.

☑ Be on the lookout for wild animals, especially poisonous snakes that may have been swept in.

☑ Be aware that flooding and debris flows can follow a hurricane, some-times hours or even days after a storm event. Monitor news stations for flood reports.

What Not To Do

☑ Do not go outside.

☑ Do not stand or crouch near windows or doors.

☑ Do not leave interior doors open; they can swing loose and become hazards.

☑ If you live in a high-rise, do not take the elevator to lower floors; use the stairs.

☑ Do not use your phone unless it's urgent. This will prevent logjams on telephone lines and free up "space" for emergency calls.

☑ Do not light any candles. This could ignite any gas present. Flashlight bat-teries could also ignite leaking gas, if present. Step outside to turn your flashlight on, or do so before reentering your home if you evacuated.

☑ After the storm, do not drink or prepare food with tap water until you are sure it's not contaminated.

Flood Safety

How to Prepare

What To Do

☑ Check flood-hazard maps to evaluate the risk of flooding in your area. Use FEMA's website (floodsmart.gov) for information and resources.

☑ Determine what type of flood insurance you may need. The less the risk of flood to your home, the lower the cost of flood insurance.

☑ Put together an emergency kit and establish an evacuation plan with family members. Consider conducting flood drills.

☑ Construct flood barriers; seal and waterproof basement walls and windows. Help build flood barriers along your community's levees or riverbanks as able—and directed by officials.

☑ Consider installing backflow valves to prevent water from backing up in your water system during a flood.

☑ Be aware of your proximity to streams, drainage channels, canyons, and other low-lying areas that are known to flood.

☑ Study water-flow patterns around your home during lighter rains to see if there are spots where water pools or drains toward your house.

☑ Bring any outside furniture indoors or tie it down securely.

☑ Keep a battery-powered radio and your phone charged at all times.

What Not To Do

☑ Do not ignore the risk of floods, even if you live in an area that is not predisposed to flooding; floods can happen almost anywhere.

☑ Do not build in a floodplain without taking precautions to elevate and reinforce your home.

☑ Do not plan to be in areas that have been scorched by fire if precipitation threatens; floods can occur more easily on burnt ground, which doesn't absorb water well.

☑ If you are planning on camping or hiking, do not head for valleys or low-lying areas during wet seasons.

How to Stay Safe

What To Do

☑ Be on the alert for disaster sirens.

☑ Stay tuned to weather and flood reports on the radio, television, or your smartphone.

☑ Evacuate immediately if there is any possibility of flash floods occurring.

☑ Move important items to an upper floor, and secure your home before evacuating.

☑ Turn off electricity at central switches and close off the gas at main valves.

☉ If water is already rising inside your home, go upstairs to a higher floor, to the attic, or even onto the roof.

☑ Clean your hands often with soap and disinfected water or with hand sanitizer, especially if you have come into contact with floodwater.

☑ If you are driving as floodwater rises around your car, stop the car and get out.

☑ Use a stick or other nonconducting object to check that the ground in front of you is safe to walk on.

☑ Move to higher ground.

☑ Use extreme caution when returning home after evacuation. Structural damage can be serious but hidden from view.

☑ Check the integrity of porches, roofs, and overhangs for stability. Check outside for loose or downed power lines, broken gas lines, and any damage to your foundation. Sniff for natural or propane gas, and listen for any hissing noises indicating a leak.

☑ Look out for any wild animals, especially reptiles, that may have washed into your home.

What Not To Do

☑ If there is no choice but to walk through water, walk where the water is not moving. Just six inches of flowing water can force you to fall down.

☑ Do not approach downed power lines or anything electrical. Water conducts electricity, which means you could be electrocuted even without touching a power line.

☑ Never touch electrical wiring or equipment if you are wet.

Winter Weather Safety

How to Prepare

What To Do

☑ Be sure you have working flashlights and backup batteries.

☑ Set your home temperature to no lower than 55°F if you decide to leave your home. This will keep pipes from freezing.

☑ Tighten up weather stripping, and caulk leaks around windows, doors, and vent openings throughout your house or apartment.

☑ Look for signs or problems typical of older roofs: reroofing (three or more layers of shingles) or insulation installed without proper ventilation. Consider repair or renovation to withstand heavy snow accumulation.

☑ Winterize your car. Check antifreeze level. Be sure the battery is strong and the battery terminals are clean. Check the windshield wipers and top off windshield washer fluid. Be sure your tires are roadworthy for the sort of winter driving your area will require.

☑ Purchase a snow shovel and salt for ice melting in advance of winter storm season.

☑ Turn off the water to your outside hoses. Snow, ice, and freezing cold can split them.

What Not To Do

☑ Do not let your pipes freeze. When extremely cold temperatures are expected, leave taps open slightly so they drip. Keep indoor temperatures warm. Open kitchen cabinet doors beneath the sink.

☑ Do not let your cell phone charge drop too low. There may come a time when you cannot charge it at the wall for a while.

☑ Do not let your car's gas tank go under half full. Keep your car fueled up so you don't get caught at home needing to fill up during a blizzard.

☑ Do not ignore warnings when you hear them. Remember that a Winter Storm Watch means storm conditions are predicted within the next two to three days, while a Winter Storm Warning or Blizzard Warning means storm conditions have been observed and are imminent.

How to Stay Safe

What To Do

☑ When you are using portable heaters such as those that use kerosene, ensure there is adequate ventilation to avoid any buildup of toxic fumes. When you refuel kerosene heaters, make sure that you are outside and at least three feet from flammable objects.

☑ If your water pipes freeze, remove their insulation and wrap the pipes in rags. After you open all the faucets in your house, pour hot water over the rags and pipes.

☑ If you find yourself without power or heat, consider moving temporarily to a designated public shelter. To find the nearest one, text SHELTER followed by your zip code (for example, SHELTER 12345) to 43362 (4FEMA).

☑ Shovel walkways and driveways as soon as possible—even during periods of lighter snowfall—to expose the ground and capture sunlight. The warmth will melt remaining snow and keep ice from forming.

☑ If you are driving, stay alert and reduce distractions.

☑ If forced to pull off the road, put on your hazard lights, but conserve the car's battery by turning the lights off periodically.

☑ Start your engine and let it run with the heater on for 10 minutes every hour. Charge your phone during that period as well. Before you turn on the engine, make sure the exhaust pipe is clear of snow and debris.

☑ Open one window a crack when the engine is running.

☑ At night, turn the inside light on so rescuers can see you.

☑ Take turns staying awake if you are with others, and huddle for warmth. Move your body as much as you can to maintain body heat.

What Not To Do

☑ Do not use a generator, camp stove, or other gas- or charcoal-burning heating device inside. Carbon monoxide from these sources can be deadly.

☑ If you must travel, do so during the daytime and stay on main roads. Avoid back-road shortcuts.

☑ Do not slam on your brakes. Slow down to a stop instead. Do not change lanes or try to pass other drivers.

Emergency Websites

Keep these websites bookmarked on your computer for easy access in an emergency.

Stay Ready An informative site designed by FEMA to educate and empower Americans to prepare for and respond to emergencies including natural and human-made disasters. Available in Spanish and English. www.ready.gov

Regional Extreme Weather Information Sheets For states and regions most vulnerable to hurricanes—East Coast, Gulf Coast, and Hawaii—phone numbers and websites are updated annually.
www.ncddc.noaa.gov/activities/weather-ready-nation/newis/

Responding to Natural Disasters Fourteen types of disasters are described, including dangers and how to face them, based on the experience of FEMA officials.
www.ready.gov/natural-disasters

Finding Shelter During Disaster Maps out Red Cross shelters within your vicinity, updated every 30 minutes in response to urgent local needs.
www.redcross.org/find-help/shelter

Safe and Well Message Board The Red Cross operates a website designed as a central communication method for people to communicate with loved ones during disasters. You must register ahead to use it. It operates 24 hours a day, 365 days a year, in English and Spanish.
www.redcross.org/find-help/contact-family/register-safe-listing

Further Resources

BOOKS

Ahrens, C. Donald. *Meteorology Today: An Introduction to Weather, Climate, and the Environment.* West Publishing Company, 2008.

Henson, Robert. *The Rough Guide to Climate Change.* (Rough Guide Reference Series). Rough Guides, 2011.

Williams, Jack. *The AMS Weather Book: The Ultimate Guide to America's Weather.* University of Chicago Press and The American Meteorological Society, 2009.

WEBSITES

American Meteorological Society
www.ametsoc.org/aboutams/index.html

American Meteorological Society's education pages
www.ametsoc.org/amsedu

Atmospheric Optics
www.atoptics.co.uk

Canadian Weatheroffice
www.weatheroffice.gc.ca/canada_e.html

Cloud Appreciation Society
www.cloudappreciationsociety.org

National Weather Association
www.nwas.org/about.php

National Weather Service JetStream Online Weather School www.srh.weather.gov/jetstream

University Corporation for Atmospheric Research Spark
www2.ucar.edu

Weatherwise magazine
www.weatherwise.org

ORGANIZATIONS

American Red Cross
www.redcross.org

American Society for the Prevention of Cruelty to Animals (ASPCA)
www.aspca.org

Centers for Disease Control and Prevention (CDC)
www.cdc.gov

Environmental Protection Agency (EPA)
www.epa.gov

Federal Emergency Management Agency (FEMA)
www.fema.gov

Insurance Institute for Business & Home Safety (IBHS)
www.disastersafety.org

Intergovernmental Panel on Climate Change (IPCC)
www.ipcc.ch

National Interagency Fire Center (NIFC)
www.nifc.gov

National Aeronautics and Space Administration (NASA)
www.nasa.gov

National Climatic Data Center (NCDC)
www.ncdc.noaa.gov

National Drought Mitigation Center (NDMC)
www.drought.unl.edu

National Drought Policy Commission (NDPC)
govinfo.library.unt.edu/drought/

National Oceanic and Atmospheric Association (NOAA)
www.noaa.gov

National Storm Damage Center
stormdamagecenter.org

National Weather Service (NWS)
www.weather.gov

National Wildlife Federation (NWF)
www.nwf.org

About the Author

JACK WILLIAMS was founding editor of the *USA TODAY* weather page in 1982 and the USATODAY.com weather section in 1995. After retiring from USA TODAY in 2005, Williams was director of public outreach for the American Meteorological Society through 2009. He continues as a fellow of the society. Williams is currently a freelance writer and is the author or coauthor of seven books, including the *National Geographic Field Guide to the Water's Edge* (2012).

About the Artist

JARED TRAVNICEK is a scientific and medical illustrator. He received his M.A. in Biological and Medical Illustration from the Johns Hopkins University School of Medicine in Baltimore, Maryland. Travnicek is a Certified Medical Illustrator and a professional member of the Association of Medical Illustrators.

ILLUSTRATIONS CREDITS

|||||||||||||||||||||||||||||||||||||||||||||||||||||||||||||||||||||||||||||||||||||||||||||||||||||||

Cover (UP), Herve Lambert/Herve-Lambert/500px; Cover (LO, L to R), Katarina Stefanovic/Getty Images; Design Pics Inc./National Geographic Creative; Glow Images, Inc/Getty Images; Jason Persoff Stormdoctor/Getty Images; Spine, Jim Reed/National Geographic Creative; Back cover (L to R), Mike Theiss/National Geographic Creative; John Eastcott and Yva Momatiuk/National Geographic Creative; RGB Ventures/SuperStock/Alamy Stock Photo; Takeshi Kitagawa/EyeEm/Getty Images; 2-3, John Eastcott and Yva Momatiuk/National Geographic Creative; 4, Carl Hanninen/Getty Images; 6, Brocreative/Shutterstock; 9, Mike Grandmaison; 10, Paul Marcellini/Paul-Marcellini.com; 12, Rene Ramos/Shutterstock; 13, Michael & Patricia Fogden/Minden Pictures/National Geographic Stock; 14, Ilya Akinshin/Shutterstock; 15, Monica Schroeder/Science Source; 16, Nemeziya/ Shutterstock; 17, Henry Lansford/Science Source; 18, Joyce Photographics/Science Source; 19, Detlev van Ravenswaay/Science Source; 20, Joyce Photographics/Science Source; 21, Robert and Jean Pollock/Science Source; 22, Adam Jones/Science Source; 23, G. R. Roberts/Science Source; 24, Science Source; 25, Gregory K. Scott/Science Source; 26, Mark Schneider/Visuals Unlimited, Inc.; 27, WimL/Shutterstock; 28, Brenda Tharp/Science Source; 29, Gregg Schieve/schievephoto.com; 30, Ralf Broskvar/Shutterstock; 31, Mike Hollingshead/Science Source; 32, Jim Reed/Science Source; 33, Jim Corwin; 34, David R. Frazier/Science Source; 35, Christophe Cadiran/Science Source; 36, Jerry Schad/Science Source; 37, Pekka Parviainen/Science Source; 38, Jim Reed/Science Source; 39, Jim W. Grace/Science Source; 40, Robert & Jean Pollock/Visuals Unlimited, Inc.; 41, Giselle Goloy; 42, Mike Hollingshead/Science Source; 43, Design Pics/Steve Nagy/Getty Images; 44, Santanor/Shutterstock; 45, David Hosking/FLPA/Minden Pictures; 46, Paul Mansfield Photography/Getty Images; 47, Kamparin/Shutterstock; 48, Stan Honda/AFP/Getty Images; 49, Daniel Friedrichs/AFP/Getty Images; 50, Tim Laman/National Geographic Stock; 51, Olga Miltsova/Shutterstock; 52, Kent Wood/Science Source; 53, Vortex 2/Science Source; 54, Howard Bluestein/Science Source; 55, Mike Hollingshead/Science Source; 56, Jim Reed/Science Source; 57, Jim Reed; 58, NOAA; 59, Anna Omelchenko/Shutterstock; 60, Chase Studio/Science Source; 61, Victor Habbick Visions/Science Source; 62, muratart/Shutterstock; 63, ajansen/iStockphoto; 64, Victor Habbick Visions/Science Source; 65, Gary Meszaros/Science Source; 66, Science Source; 67, Mike Hollingshead/Science Source; 68, Eric Nguyen/Science Source; 69, Mike Hollingshead/Science Source; 70, Howard Bluestein/Science Source; 71, Dr. Bernhard Weßling/Science Source; 72, St. Meyers/Science Source; 73, Will & Deni McIntyre/Science Source; 74, Jim Edds/Science Source; 75, Planet Observer/Science Source; 76, Kaj R. Svensson/Science Source; 77, Syd Greenberg/Science Source; 78, James Steinberg/Science Source; 79, AP Photo/Kiichiro Sato; 80, Kaj R. Svensson/Science Source; 81, Jim Reed/Science Source; 82, Bruce Roberts/Science Source; 83, Hoa-Qui/Science Source; 85, Alexey Stiop/iStockphoto; 87, Jim Edds/Science Source; 108, David Hosking/FLPA/Minden Pictures; 109, Dean Krakel II/Science Source; 110, Alan Copson/Getty Images; 111, Lowell Georgia/Science Source; 112, Carr Clifton/Minden Pictures; 113, Justin Lambert/The Image Bank/Getty Images; 114, Tony Freeman/Science Source; 115, Laurent Laveder/Science Source; 116, Mike Hollingshead/Science Source; 117, Steve Allen/Science Source; 118, Mark A. Schneider/Science Source; 119, Sebastian Saarloos; 120, Mike Hollingshead/Science Source; 121, Tim Holt/ Science Source; 122, Mike Hollingshead/Science Source; 123, Jamen Percy/ Shutterstock; 124, Vera Bradshaw/Science Source; 125, Lizzie Shepherd/Robert Harding World Imagery/Getty Images; 126, Ron Wolf/Tom Stack & Associates; 127, Mike Hollingshead/Science Source; 128, Wesley Bocxe/Science Source; 129, dotshock/Shutterstock; 130, Richard W. Brooks/Science Source; 131, Patrick Endres/Visuals Unlimited/Corbis; 132, plampy/Shutterstock; 133, Robert Jakatics/Shutterstock; 134, David R. Frazier/Science Source; 135, Jim Reed/Science Source; 136, Jim Edds/Science Source; 137, Sergiy Zavgorodny/Shutterstock; 138, Bruce M. Herman/Science Source; 139, Dariush M/Shutterstock; 140, Science Source; 141, Mark Horn/Getty Images; 142, Ted Kinsman/ Science Source; 143, 4FR/Getty Images; 144, NOAA; 145, NOAA; 146, Mike Berger/Science Source; 147, Science Source; 148, Hank Morgan/Science Source; 149, Science Source; 150, NOAA; 151, Gregory Ochocki/Science Source; 152, Noel Celis/AFP/Getty Images; 153, NOAA; 154, Mike Theiss/National Geographic/Getty Images; 155, Ken Gillespie/Getty Images; 156, Jeff Schmaltz, MODIS Rapid Response Team, NASA/GSFC; 173, Darlene Shields.

Index

Boldface indicates
illustrations.

Since 1888, the National Geographic Society has funded more than 12,000 research, exploration, and preservation projects around the world. National Geographic Partners distributes a portion of the funds it receives from your purchase to National Geographic Society to support programs including the conservation of animals and their habitats.

National Geographic Partners
1145 17th Street NW
Washington, DC 20036-4688 USA

Become a member of National Geographic and activate your benefits today at natgeo.com/jointoday.

For information about special discounts for bulk purchases, please contact National Geographic Books Special Sales: specialsales@natgeo.com

For rights or permissions inquiries, please contact National Geographic Books Subsidiary Rights: bookrights@natgeo.com

ISBN: 978-1-4262-1786-9

Printed in Hong Kong

16/THK/1

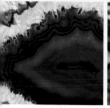

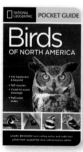

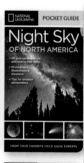
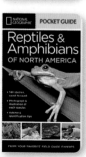
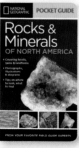
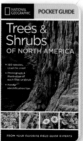